ITALY NARROW GAUGE

The Dolomites to Calabria

John Organ

Series editor Vic Mitchell

MP Middleton Press

Front Cover: Deep in Southern Italy, Borsig 0-8-0T no.353 was viewed at Camigliatello Silano with an excursion train to San Nicola-Silvano Mansio in May 2007. (P.Lawson)

Rear Cover: The constricted approach to Genoa Piazza Manin station is apparent as a former Spoleto-Norcia unit arrived with a service from Casella, whilst a trailer car awaited its next duty in the loop, in this scene recorded on 19th May 1997. (J.Wiseman)

Published May 2012

ISBN 978 1 908174 17 8

© Middleton Press, 2012

Design Deborah Esher

Published by
    Middleton Press
    Easebourne Lane
    Midhurst
    West Sussex
    GU29 9AZ
Tel: 01730 813169
Fax: 01730 812601
Email: info@middletonpress.co.uk
www.middletonpress.co.uk

Printed in the United Kingdom by Henry Ling Limited, at the Dorset Press, Dorchester, DT1 1HD

CONTENTS

1. THE DOLOMITE REGION

Val Gardena Railway	1.1 - 1.13
Rittner Bergbahn	1.14 - 1.25
Trento- Malé – Marilleva	1.26 - 1.28
Mori-Arco-Riva del Garda	1.29

2. THE SWISS CONNECTION

The Centovalli and Vigezzina	2.1 - 2.6
The RhB at Tirano	2.7 - 2.8

3. PIEDMONT and LIGURIA

Pinerola – Perosa	3.1 - 3.5
Ferrovia Genoa – Casella	3.6 - 3.17

4. THE ADRIATIC COAST and UMBRIA

Rimini – Novafeltria	4.1 - 4.2
Pescara – Penne	4.3 - 4.6
Spoleto – Norcia	4.7 - 4.11

5. ROME and NAPLES

Ferrovia Roma-Fiuggi	5.1 - 5.3
Ferrovia Alifana	5.4 - 5.6
Circumvesuviana (SFSM)	5.7 - 5.11

6. PUGLIA and CALABRIA

Bari – Barletta	6.1 - 6.2
Ferrovie Appulo-Lucane (FAL)	6.3 - 6.10
Ferrovie della Calabria (FdeC)	6.11 - 6.48

ABBREVIATIONS

CEMSA	-	Costruzioni Elettromeccanica di Saronno SpA
FAL	-	Ferrovie Appulo-Lucane
FdeC	-	Ferrovie della Calabria
FCL	-	Ferrovie Calabro-Lucane
FS	-	Ferrovie dello Stato
MCL	-	Mediterraneo Calabro-Lucane
SFSM	-	Strade Ferrate Secondarie Meridionali
SLM	-	Schweizerische Locomotiv und Maschinenfabrik, Winterthur

ACKNOWLEDGEMENTS

This publication would not have been possible without the invaluable assistance from the photographers whose work graces these pages, together with the help received in various ways from other contributors. I therefore wish to record my thanks to Alan Heywood, Tim Hills, Peter Lawson, Brian Pearce, Jean-Louis Rochaix, D.Trevor Rowe, Reinhard Todt and Jeremy Wiseman. Finally, but by no means last, I must thank my wife Brenda who has shown her usual tolerance and support during the period of research and compilation.

INTRODUCTION

In common with the majority of European countries, Italy once boasted a large assortment of narrow gauge railways. These ranged in gauges from 760mm and 1000mm in the north of the country, where the influence of the former Austro-Hungarian Empire prevailed, to the 950mm further south – a gauge more commonly associated with Italy and its satellite countries. The majority of the narrow gauge railways were independent operations. However during the inter-war period, some of the principal lines were incorporated into Ferrovie dello Stato (FS), the State Railway network formed in 1905.

Many of the lines featured in this album were electrified tramways, some of which have survived to the present time as part of urban metro systems. The traditional steam and diesel operated railways have not fared so well, only the extensive systems in the south of Italy retaining any resemblance of their former glory. Here can still be found the only remaining steam hauled services in the country, albeit on a relatively short stretch of scenic line during the summer season. Even so, a journey over these routes in a modern DMU can be quite an exhilarating experience in an area where steep gradients and lofty viaducts abound.

This album will concentrate mainly on the historical aspect of the subject, portraying many splendid systems that have succumbed to the "march of progress". The modern image of the surviving lines has not been overlooked, with more recent views to bring the survey up to date.

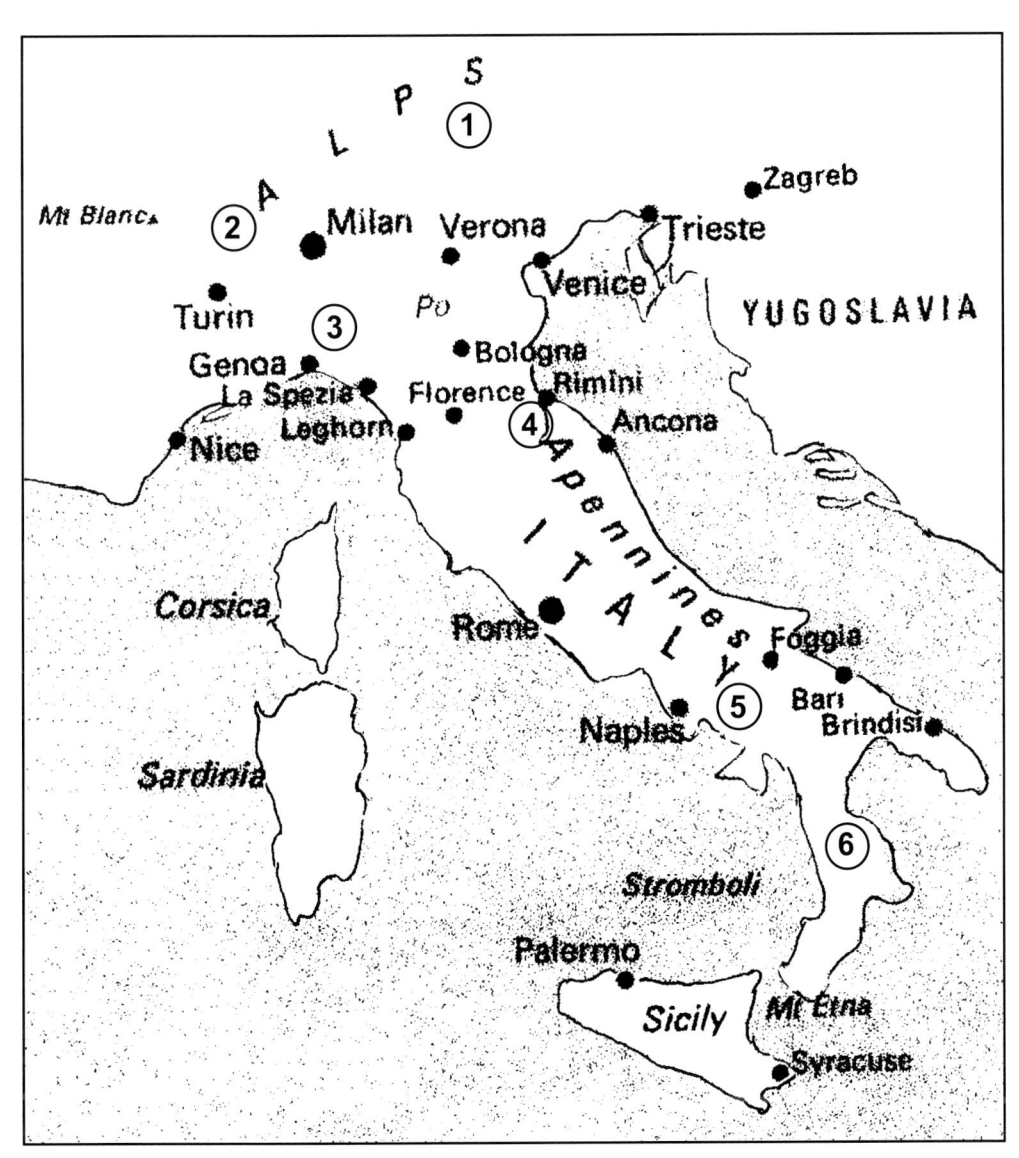

I. The distinctive outline of the Italian peninsula showing the location of the railways featured in this volume. The numbers refer to the relative section headings.

1. The Dolomite Region

The area in the northeast of Italy was formerly part of the Austro-Hungarian Empire, a consequence of which is that the German language is still widely spoken and many towns and villages in the region have bi-lingual names. Still known by its Austrian name of the South Tyrol, the area is dominated by the Dolomite range of mountains, the craggy red limestone peaks that are unique to this part of the European mainland. The area was a hotly disputed territory during World War One, being ceded to Italy following the Armistice in 1918.

Four principal narrow gauge railways were once a notable feature of this mountainous region, of which only one has survived in its entirety. Sadly the others have succumbed, of which one in particular would have been a notable tourist attraction had it survived a little longer. For the purpose of this publication, the place names used in this bi-lingual area are the Italian variant, with the German name, where applicable, in brackets – some of which bear little resemblance to each version!

VAL GARDENA RAILWAY

II. The route of the sadly missed Val Gardena Railway (also known in German as the Grödenbahn), showing its vital connection to the Brenner Pass line. (J.M.Jarvis)

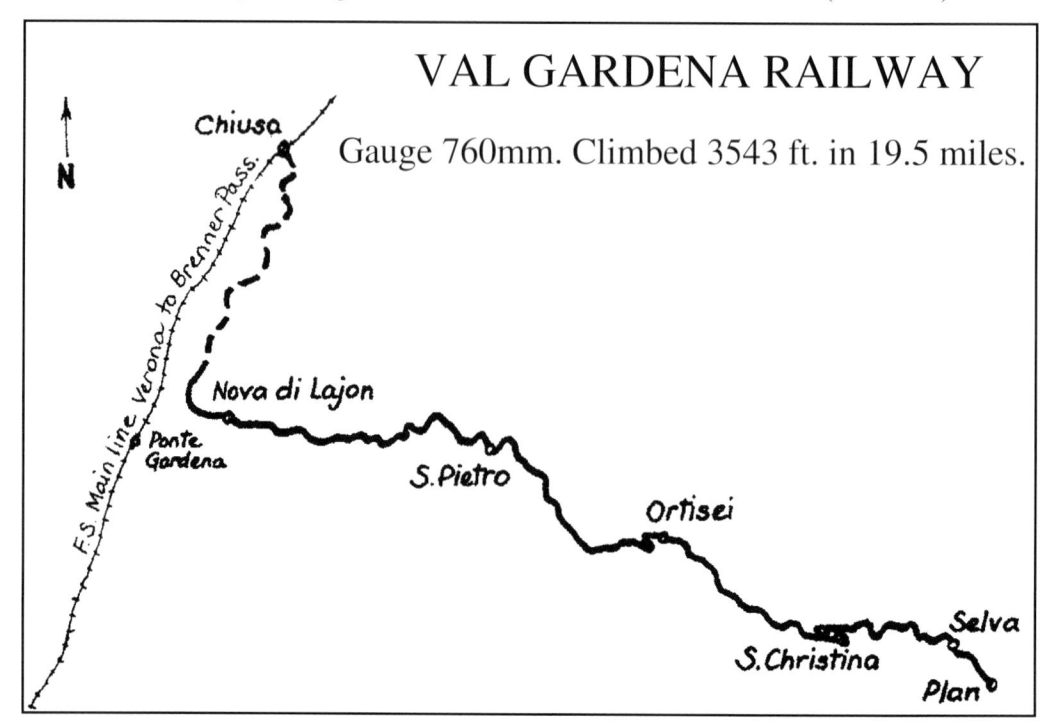

VAL GARDENA RAILWAY
Gauge 760mm. Climbed 3543 ft. in 19.5 miles.

Chiusa
Nova di Lajon
Ponte Gardena
S. Pietro
Ortisei
S. Christina
Selva
Plan
F.S. Main line Verona to Brenner Pass.

Originally constructed in 1916 by the Austrian military forces to provide a means of access from the main artery of the Brenner Pass route to the hotly fought strongholds in the Dolomite Mountains, this 32.5km long 760mm gauge line was transferred to the Italian State Railways (FS) in 1919 and adapted to its new role as a public railway.

The line began its sinuous route from Chiusa (Klausen), situated on the main line linking Innsbruck and Verona. The route initially headed south before veering to the east and climbing on a ruling grade of 1 in 20 via Ortisei and Santa Christina to the upper terminus at Plan, at an altitude of 1613m, having climbed 1093m from Chiusa. As well as the twisting nature of the route, including a double hairpin above Santa Christiana, nine tunnels were negotiated during the initial part of the highly scenic journey.

Being built by Austria, it not surprisingly featured many attributes commonly found on the 760mm gauge railways that were prevalent further north in the former empire. As a consequence, motive power was supplied by a fleet of seven K class 0-8-0WT locomotives built by Krauss of Linz for the opening of the line in 1916. Re-numbered R410-001 – R410-007 by FS following its absorption into the Italian network, these remained the only machines employed on the line during its entire life of which five examples survived until closure. Nos R410-002 and 007 were drafted to Yugoslavia in 1942, from where they never returned. The only survivor is no.R410-005, which has been preserved on a plinth near to the former upper terminus.

Having survived the rigours of another war between 1939 and 1945, the line was eventually overtaken by a vast improvement to the road network that was implemented during the 1950s. The competition from road transport proved to be untenable, with the result that this fascinating railway was closed in 1960. Unfortunately, the closure occurred at a time that the area was being developed as a major tourist and winter sports destination. Had more foresight been given to the situation and the line retained for a little longer, it could well have featured in the future plans for the region and become a major tourist attraction in its own right.

1.1. The distinctive lines of a Krauss K Class 0-8-0WT were seen to advantage in this view of no.R 410-001 at Chiusa in June 1959. The viaduct carrying the FS Brenner main line is visible in the background. (R.Todt / BVA)

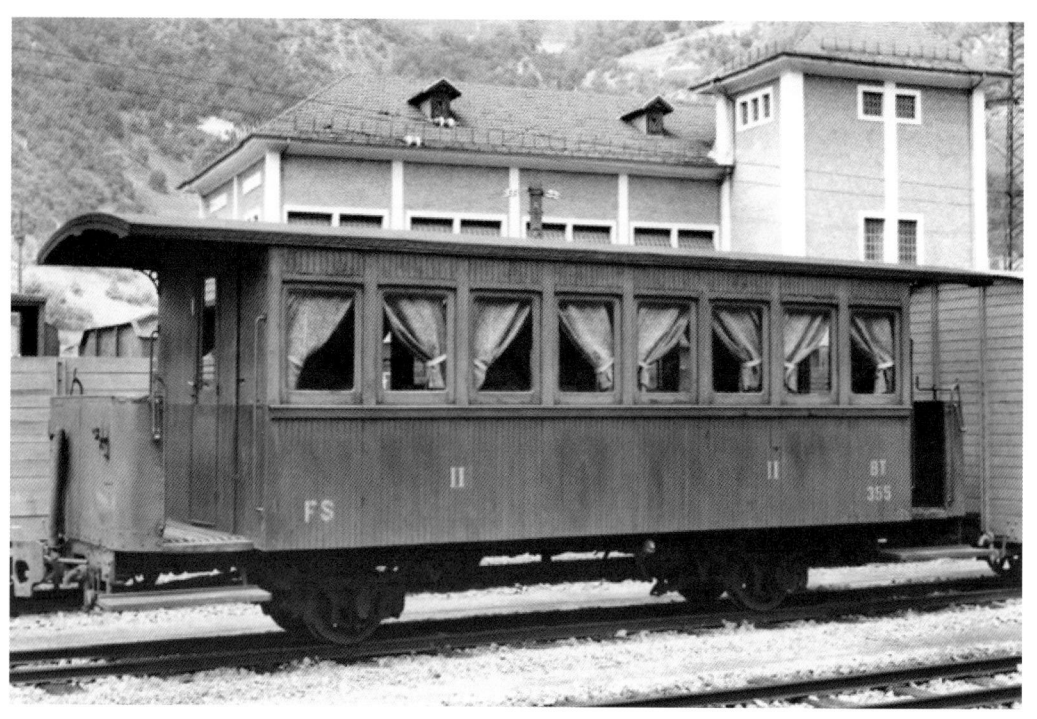

1.2. On the same occasion, one of the typical Austrian balcony ended 4 wheel carriages, no.BT 355, was photographed in the station at Chiusa. (R.Todt / BVA)

1.3. Also viewed at Chiusa in June 1959 was this splendid parcels van attached to the rear of a train being prepared for a journey to Plan. (R.Todt / BVA)

1.4. The train seen in the previous scene, with no.R 410-001 at its head, was replenishing its water tank supply at S.Pietro when it was photographed in June 1959. (R.Todt / BVA)

1.5. During the course of a return journey from Plan, the Krauss 0-8-0WT was witnessed at Ortisei (St.Ulrich), with the typical Alpine buildings in the background, on the same occasion during June 1959. (R.Todt / BVA)

1.6. No.R 410-004 was viewed as it passed no.R 410-005 at Ortisei, whilst en-route to Plan on 15th September 1959. (D.Trevor Rowe)

1.7. Another Alpine village at S.Christina was the location of a further water stop for no.R410-001, during the course of its journey from Chiusa to Plan in June 1959. (R.Todt / BVA)

1.8   The same train was recorded at S.Christina from the opposite side of the station. Note the insulation for the water column and the hose being fed to the water filler for the well tank, situated inside the cab of the locomotive. (R.Todt / BVA)

1.9   During the final stages of the climb to Plan, the train hauled by no.R 410-001 pauses at a wayside halt on the same occasion. (R.Todt / BVA)

1.10. With the imposing peaks of the Dolomites in the background, the Krauss well-tank locomotive was witnessed as it was about to depart from Plan with a return descent to Chiusa during June 1959. (R.Todt / BVA)

1.11. A detailed view of no. R 410-001 was obtained at Plan on the same occasion. Despite being fitted with well tanks, the design of the locomotive has all the hallmarks of the products of the Krauss (Linz) works. (R. Todt / BVA)

1.12. Sister locomotive no. R 410-004 was recorded at Plan as it departed for Chiusa, with a typical formation of three carriages and a parcels van, on 15th September 1959.
(D. Trevor Rowe)

1.13. Our final view of the much lamented Val Gardena Railway features no.R 410-004, which was witnessed outside the single road shed at Plan, shortly after arrival from Chiusa on the same date. (D.Trevor Rowe)

RITTNER BERGBAHN

The principal town of the Dolomite region is Bolzano (Bozen). This attractive town, situated at the southern end of the Brenner Pass route between Italy and Austria, has become a major centre for the tourist industry that has taken a stronghold in the area. Situated between the Dolomites to the east and the southern flanks of the Alps to the west, it is ideally located for its role as a holiday destination in both summer and winter.

In 1907 a steeply graded metre gauge railway was constructed to connect the centre of Bolzano to the Ritten plateau, 990m above the town to the northeast. The line commenced from the terminus shared with the town tramway system at Walther Platz. The two systems used a common route for a short distance before the Rittner Bergbahn tracks diverted onto a Strub system rack and pinion incline 5.5km in length on an average gradient of 1 in 4. The summit of the climb was reached at L'Assunta (Maria Himmelfaht) from which the line continued for a further 6.6km on an adhesion section with a gentle gradient of 1 in 200 to the upper terminus at Collalbo (Klobenstein). On the rack section the trains were propelled by a rack fitted locomotive, this also being used to assist with the braking of a descending train. The electric current was 750 volts DC from an overhead system.

During the 1960s a new road was built from Bolzano to the Ritten plateau, which provided a faster alternative route. However, the future of the rack section was compromised following a serious accident in 1966, the cause of which was as a result of reduced maintenance to the track. This resulted in the rack section being closed and replaced by an aerial cable car. This connects with the upper section of the line at Soprabolzano (Oberbozen) which continues to operate between L'Assunta and Collalbo, although the 1.1km section between L'Assunta and Soprabolzano is little used. The surviving section is now mainly operated with tramcars obtained secondhand from Germany in 1982 and Switzerland in 2009. However some of the original 1907 stock remains in service whilst other examples, including a rack fitted locomotive, are displayed at the Tiroler Museumsbahnen in Innsbruck.

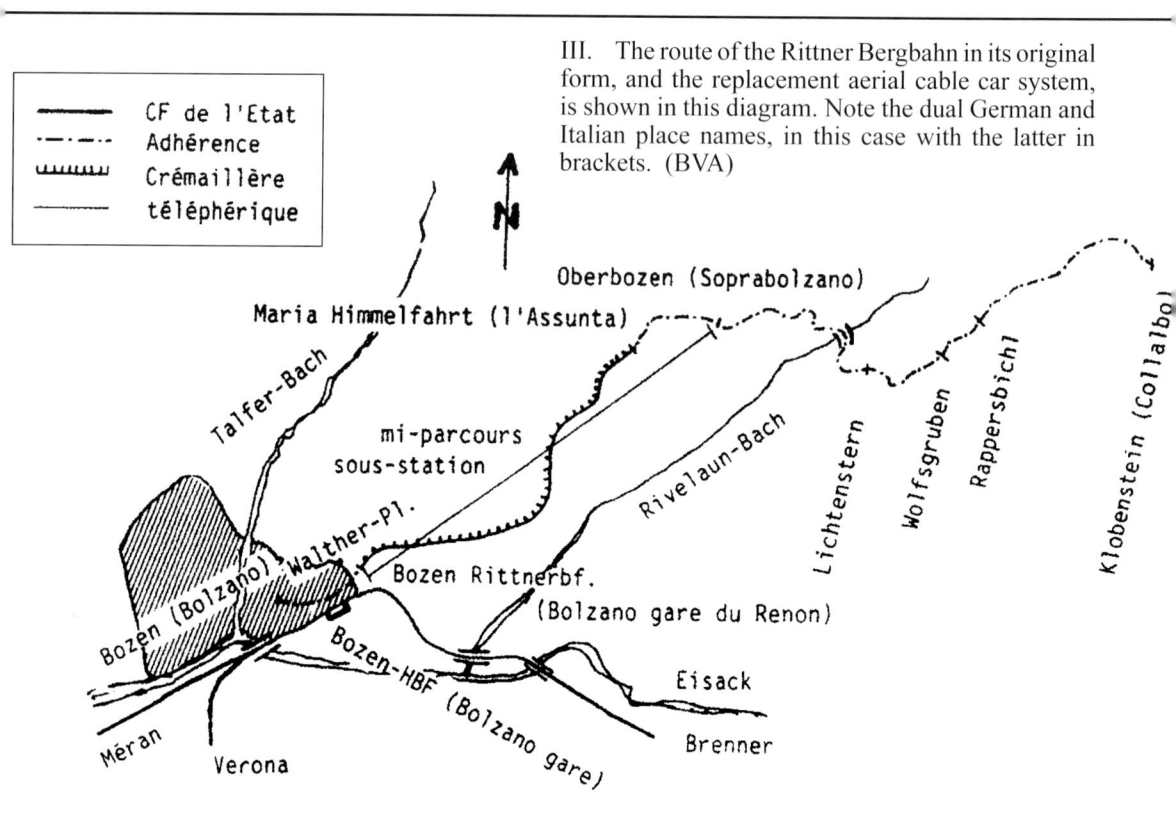

III. The route of the Rittner Bergbahn in its original form, and the replacement aerial cable car system, is shown in this diagram. Note the dual German and Italian place names, in this case with the latter in brackets. (BVA)

1.14. A 750v DC electric car of the Rittner Bergbahn was recorded at Walther Platz in Bolzano (Bozen) prior to departure for Collabo (Klobenstein) in April 1954. (R.Todt / BVA)

1.15. A rack fitted locomotive propelled a single tramcar and two wagons, whilst ascending the Strub system incline between Bolzano and L'Assunta (Maria Himmelfaht), when this scene was photographed during May 1960. (R.Todt /BVA)

1.16. No. L3, the locomotive seen in the previous scene, was the principal subject of this view of the same train ascending the incline. (R.Todt /BVA)

1.17. At the summit of the incline the Swiss built locomotive, one of four built by SLM in 1907, waited in the loop at L'Assunta prior to assisting with the braking for a train on the return journey to Bolzano. (R.Todt / BVA)

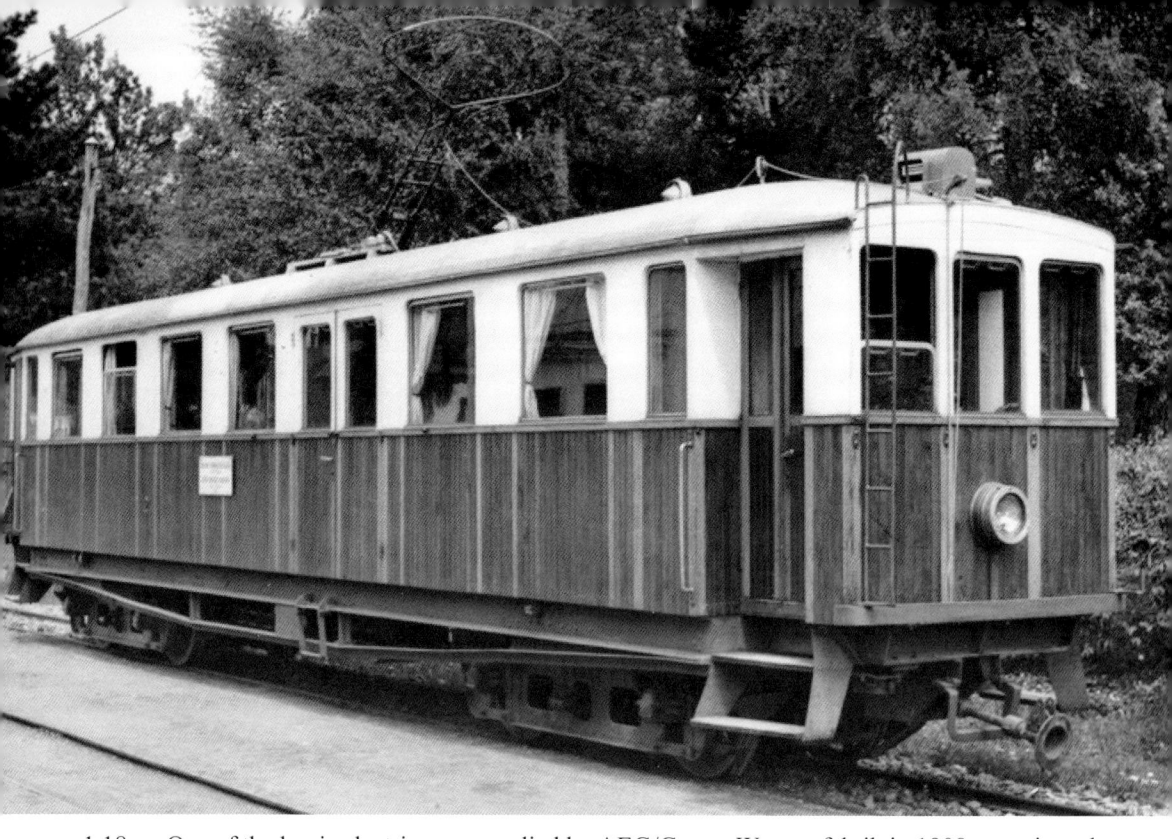

1.18. One of the bogie electric cars supplied by AEG/Grazer Waggonfabrik in 1908 was viewed at L'Assunta in May 1960. (R.Todt /BVA)

1.19. With the summit of the Strub system incline in the distance, a locomotive propelled train has just arrived from Bolzano at L'Assunta on the same occasion.
(R.Todt / BVA)

1.20. Within a short time, the locomotive had been attached to the front of another single car unit, prior to the descent of the incline to Bolzano. (R.Todt /BVA)

1.21. At Soprabolzano (Oberbozen) on the adhesion section of the route, the AEG motor car propelled a single wagon on the final stage of the journey to the upper summit of the line, in another scene witnessed during May 1960. (R.Todt /BVA)

1.22.   The attractive station building at Soprabolzano is also featured in this view of the same train as seen in the previous scene. (R.Todt /BVA)

1.23.   High on the Ritten Plateau, a unit destined for Collalbo (Klobenstein) was photographed as it approached a footpath crossing in May 1979. (R.Todt /BVA)

1.24. The same 1907-built electric motor-car was viewed as it arrived at the terminus of the Rittnerbahn at Collalbo during May 1979. (R.Todt /BVA)

1.25. Built to a similar design as the AEG electric bogie units, two trailer cars were also supplied in 1907. No. B21 was photographed at Collalbo in May 1960. (R.Todt /BVA)

TRENTO-MALÉ- MARILLEVA

To the south of Bolzano is the town of Trento, which is situated between the Alps and the Italian lakes. In 1909 a metre gauge railway was constructed to connect Trento with Malé, 56km to the north. The line was electrified from the outset at 800 volts DC and originally operated by the local transport authority. In 1936 it was incorporated into the state system (FS) until 1945 when it was transferred to a newly formed public company Societá Locale Trento-Malé. The operation remained virtually unchanged until 1964 when a renovation programme took place, which included converting the electrical supply to 3000 volts DC. In 2002 the line was incorporated once again into the Trento transport authority, which immediately extended it a further 10km to the developing ski-resort of Marilleva. The Ferrovia Trento-Malé-Marilleva (FTM) is now a very profitable undertaking, carrying over 2 million passengers annually along its 66km route.

1.26.   A train bound for Malé is seen as it departed from Trento towards the mountains in the background. This scene at the extensive station complex was recorded on 29th December 1975. (J.Wiseman)

1.27. At Malé a two-car EMU no.18 is pictured alongside the depot during May 2000. Note the immaculate condition of the permanent way. (A.Heywood)

➔ 1.28. The same EMU set was recorded as it arrived at Malé, shortly after the line had been extended to Marilleva. This view of the upper section of the route was obtained on 21st May 2004. (J.Wiseman)

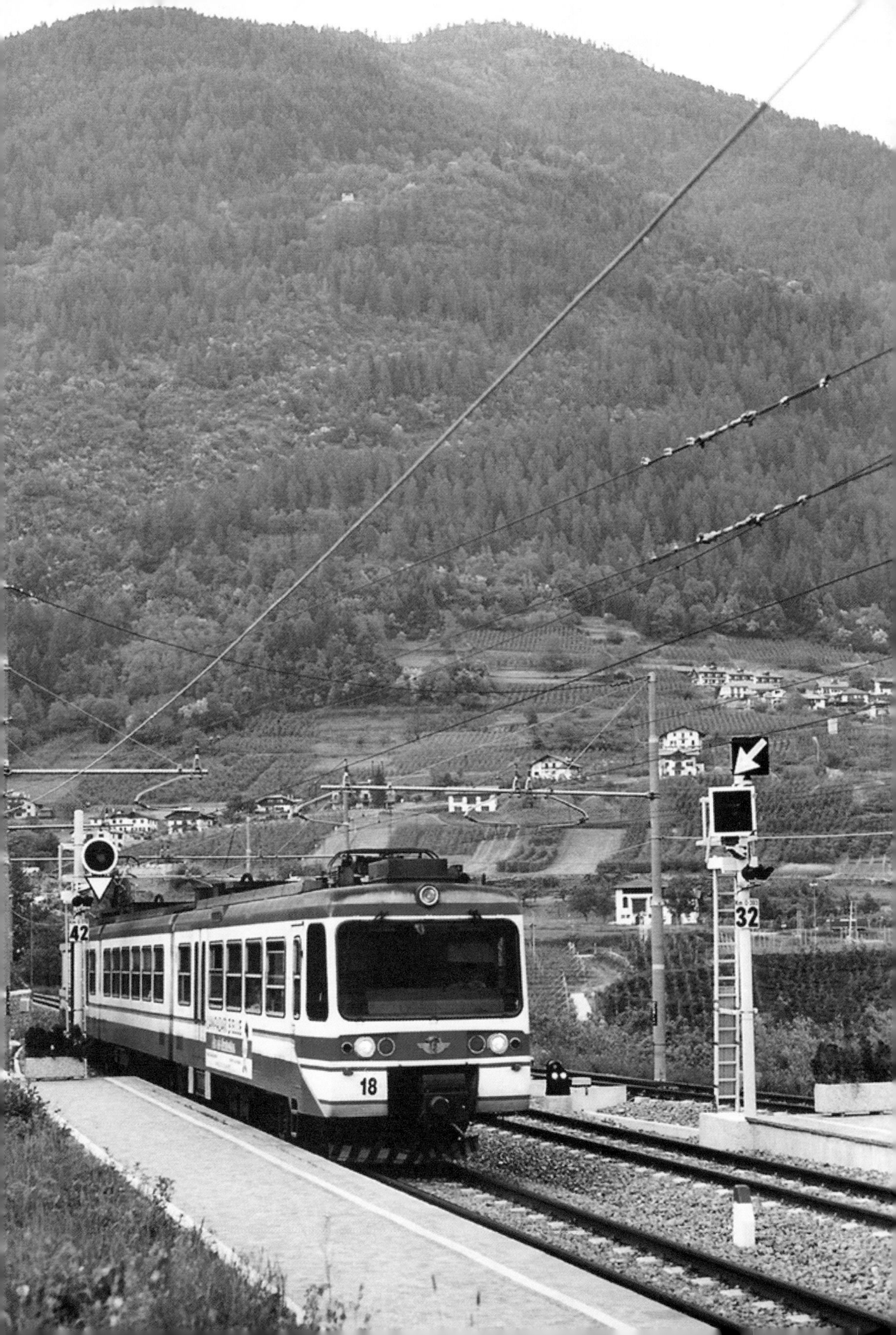
42
32
18

MORI-ARCO-RIVA del GARDA

The first narrow gauge railway to be constructed in the South Tyrol dates from 1890, when a 760mm line was laid to connect the Innsbruck to Verona main line at Rovereto with Riva, situated at the northern head of Lake Garda. The 24km long line was built as a passenger operation in order to convey tourists to the lakeside attractions, although freight was also carried. Sadly the line suffered heavy damage during World War One and was closed following the end of hostilities.

The motive power for the railway was provided by three 0-6-2Ts built by Krauss (Linz) in 1890 to the same design as those supplied to other Austrian lines during the same period. In 1915, one of the locomotives (no.2 *Riva*) was drafted to the military railways in Hungary to assist with the war effort. This move was fortunate in that it ultimately secured its future survival. Between 1918 and 1941 *Riva* worked at an industrial railway in Poland, whilst another stint of military service beckoned during WW2. From 1945 until 1968, *Riva* worked in Romania where it was in regular use as CFR no.395-104 on the Alba Iulia-Zlatna line (see *Romania & Bulgaria Narrow Gauge*). Following its retirement from active service, the locomotive was stored at an industrial site until it was acquired in 1974 by the Omaha Zoo Railway and exported to the USA, where it is still in regular use.

IV. This sketch shows the route of this long defunct railway. The connection with the FS Brenner Pass route is again featured. (Transpress)

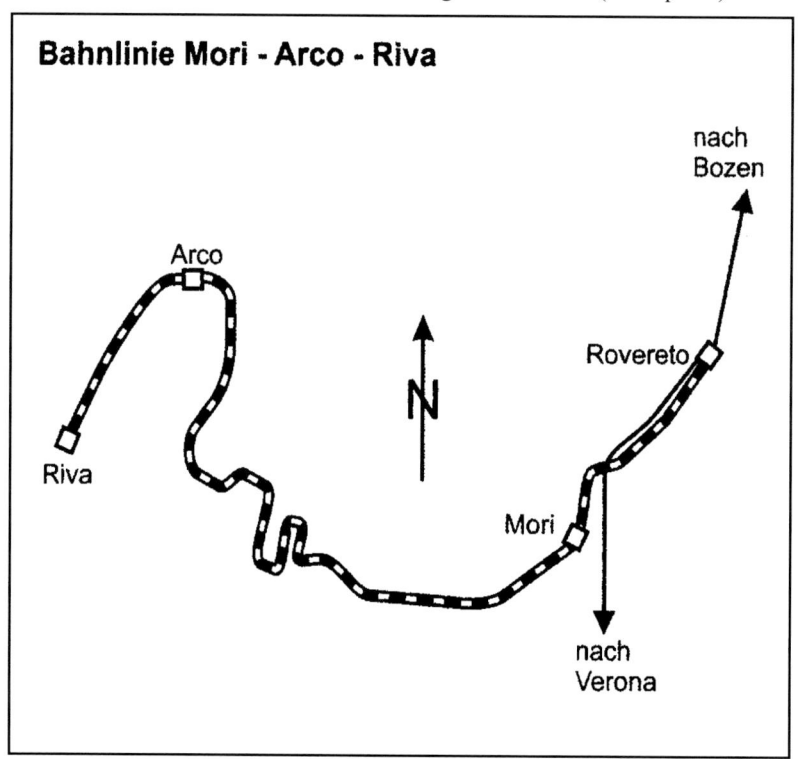

1.29. The sole surviving Krauss 0-6-2T of the Mori-Arco-Riva line, no.2 *Riva* worked for many years in Romania prior to its emigration to the USA. The well travelled locomotive was viewed at Alba Iulia during September 1966. (D.Trevor Rowe)

2. The Swiss Connection

The Alpine region of northwest Italy is intertwined with Switzerland, the border following a curvaceous route through the southern flanks of the mountains. Notable for its lakes set in stupendous scenic locations, the area is home to an international narrow gauge railway jointly operated by companies from both countries. In addition, the largest of the Swiss metre gauge lines has its southern terminus on Italian soil.

The CENTOVALLI and VIGEZZINA Railway

This international metre gauge railway is jointly operated by the Italian Società Subalpina di Imprese Ferroviarie S.P.A. (SSIF) and the Swiss Ferrovie Autolinee Regionali Ticinesi (FART). The 53km long line, of which 33km is in Italy, was opened in 1923 and operates on an overhead electrical supply of 1200 volts DC. The line connects with the Simplon route at its western terminus at Domodossola , whilst the eastern terminus is at Locarno. Here a connection with the Gotthard route is made via a standard gauge branch line to Bellinzona. The border between the two countries is at Camedo, although the limited customs procedures are carried out at the two terminal stations or on board the trains.

Prior to the construction of the Furka Base Tunnel in 1982, the Centovalli line assumed great importance as it was the only rail route traversing the Swiss and Italian Alps in an East-West direction that remained open during the winter months. Although the Furka route has now absorbed much of this traffic, the line still provides an essential service to the area in the south of the mountain chain.

The route is one of great scenic charm as it crosses innumerable valleys on lofty viaducts, notably on the Italian section to the west, where many watercourses descend from the Alps before draining onto the northern plains of Italy. At Locarno, the former attractive lakeside approach to the terminus has since 1992 been replaced by a subterranean route to an underground station situated below the SBB standard gauge terminus. The line has always been operated by articulated EMU sets. The original two- car units were replaced between 1959 and 1968 by a fleet of nine vehicles split between the two operating companies. These were largely superseded by 12 modernised two-car sets in 1992, whilst in 2007 they were joined by three four-car panoramic sets which have proved very popular with the heavy amount of tourist traffic which the line attracts. Although traversing Italian soil for more than half its length, the line accepts Swiss Travel Passes for the entire journey, which makes it an essential part of any railway holiday to Switzerland.

V.   The international route between Domodossola in Italy and Locarno in Switzerland is shown in this map of the area, with its connections to the Simplon route at Domodossola and the St.Gotthard route at Bellinzona.

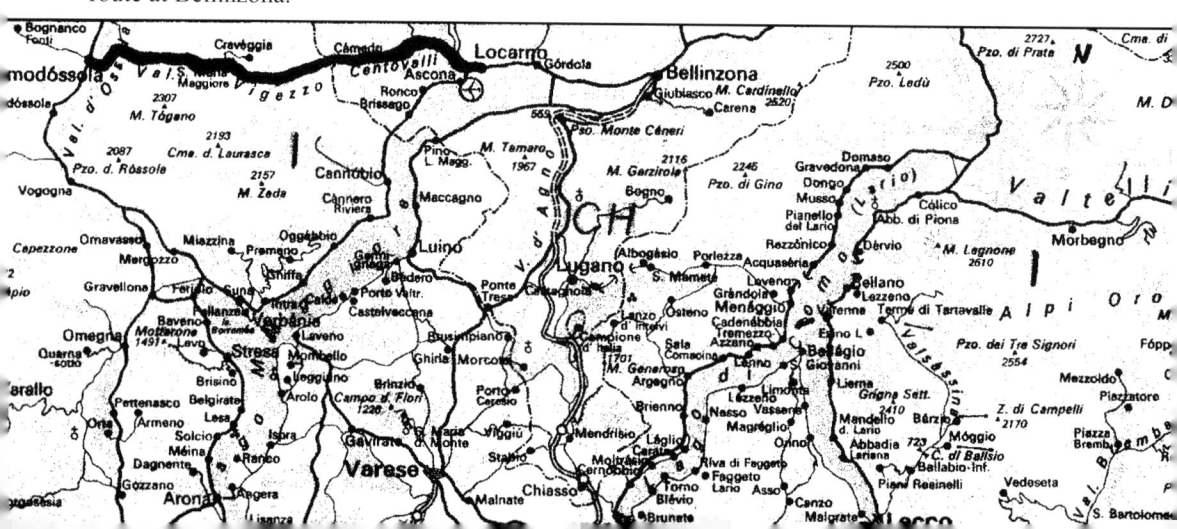

2.1.   A former Locarno urban tram is seen alongside the goods shed at Domodossola, along with some freight wagons, on 14th September 1965. (J.Wiseman)

2.2.   The Centovalli personified. A train crosses one of the many viaducts to be found on the route as it approached Domodossola during the final stage of its journey from Locarno on 14th April 1991. (J.Wiseman)

2.3.　　　The typically Alpine station at Santa Maria Maggiore dominates this view of another vintage tram car on 30th June 1980. (J.Wiseman)

➔ 2.4.　　　Photographed from a train bound for Locarno, the passing loop at Malesco was the location for this record of a Domodossola bound train entering the station during May 2000. (A.Heywood)

➔ 2.5.　　At the same location, the westbound train was recorded as it left the station and headed towards Domodossola. (A.Heywood)

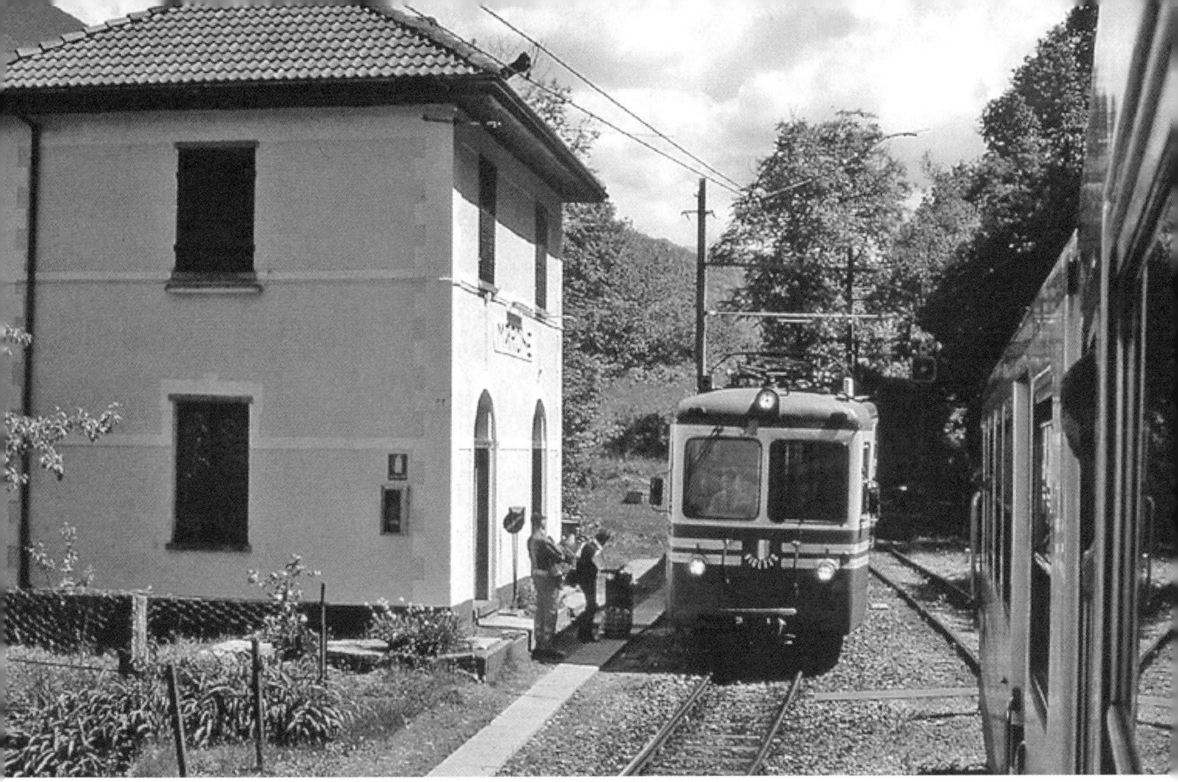

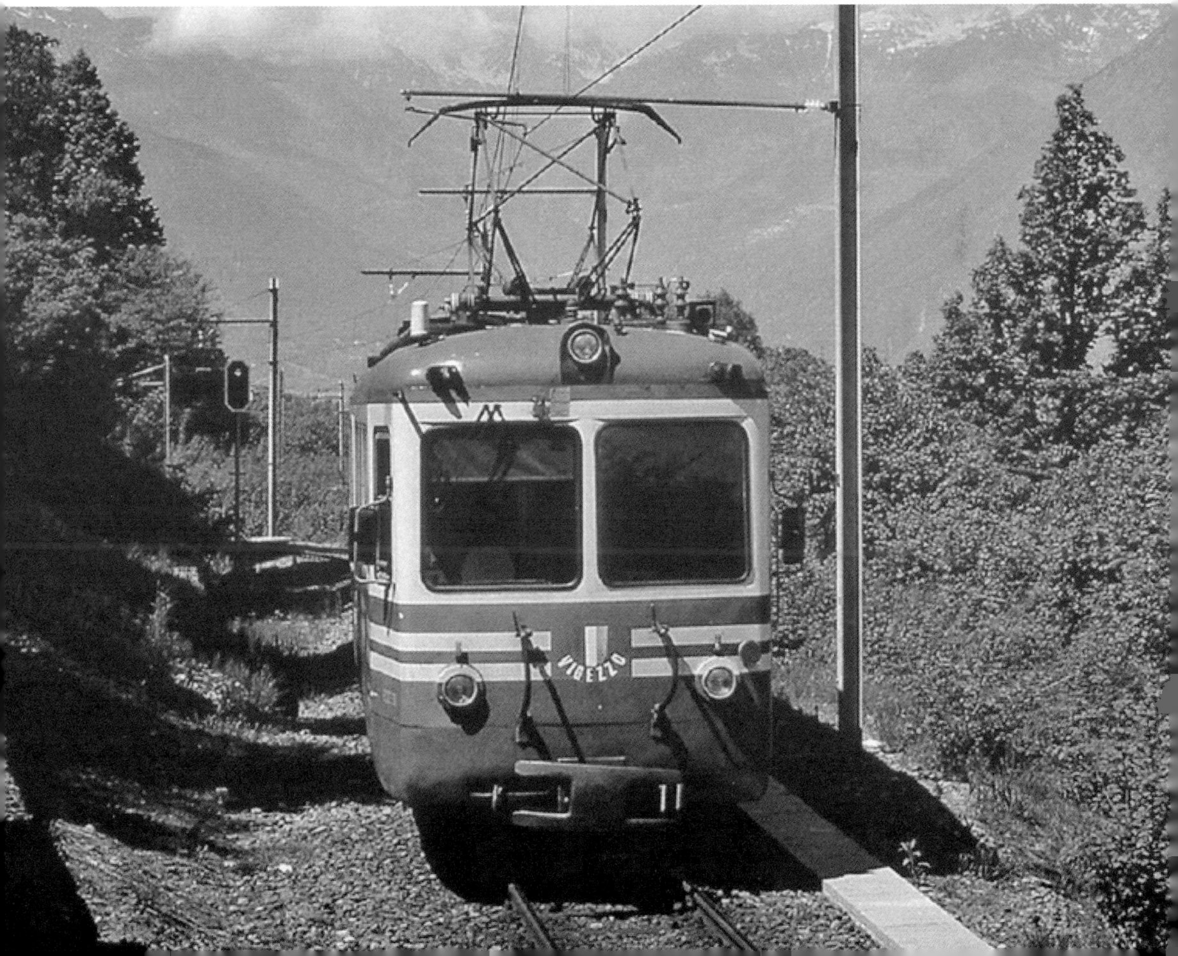
VIGEZZO
11

2.6. Near the Swiss border at Re, a plethora of trains were gathered whilst passengers were transferred to the buses on the left of the photograph. Due to the line in Switzerland being blocked following an un-seasonal landslide, the buses were in use for the section between Re and Locarno on 30th June 1980. (J.Wiseman)

The RhB at TIRANO

The Bernina Bahn was opened in 1910 between St. Moritz and the Italian border town of Tirano. In 1942 it was absorbed by the Rhätische Bahn (RhB), thus producing the largest independent railway in Switzerland (see *Swiss Narrow Gauge*). The route passes into Italy at Campocologno, 4km from the southern terminus. From the border, which is marked by a pair of rusty gates which haven't been shut for many years (probably not since 1945!), the line passes through the suburbs of Tirano before traversing the main square of the town. The terminus is at a joint station shared with a FS standard gauge branch line from Milan. Always a busy route due to the scenic attractions of the line through southern Switzerland, it also provides a useful connection with the Italian main line network. The journey time from Tirano to Milan is around 2 hours, thus providing the area traversed by the RhB with a convenient route to the heartland of northern Italy.

2.7. Viewed from the FS standard gauge platform at Tirano, two RhB trainsets were recorded in the metre gauge terminus of the Swiss line during February 1985. (J.F.Organ)

2.8. Here is a characteristic Swiss railway scene witnessed in Italy. An RhB train from St. Moritz was viewed as it arrived at Tirano, whilst a wagon loaded with timber awaits shipment alongside, on 25th September 1989. (J.F.Organ)

3. Piedmont and Liguria

These regions in the northwest of Italy are located in a very scenic area, much of which is set within the southern flanks of the Alpine range. They are also dominated by the industrial city of Turin and the extensive coastal port of Genoa respectively. Although the area has possessed little in the way of narrow gauge railways, it once boasted one of the earliest lines to be constructed in the country. At the other extreme one of the more scenic of the Italian lines has survived to provide an essential service to the locality it serves, with a seemingly guaranteed future.

PINEROLA - PEROSA

During the late 19th Century, means of communication in the rural areas of Italy were, in common with much of Europe, limited to say the least. One particular region was in Piedmont to the west of Turin. The two towns of Pinerola and Perosa were particularly in need of some form of connection. As a consequence a tramway, 12km in length, was opened in 1881 and built to the unusual gauge of 1100mm. The reason for this choice of gauge was dictated by the use of redundant track and fixtures from the short lived Mount Cenis Railway. This had been constructed by J.B.Fell in 1868 using the 1100mm gauge and his patented Fell system to provide a cross Alpine route between France and Italy. With the opening of the Mount Cenis Tunnel in 1871, the mountain route was abandoned resulting in the availability of much 1100mm track material.

Known originally as the Piedmont Steam Tramway, the newly laid line provided an invaluable service between the two towns. In 1928 it was modernised and electrified, although it still retained its unusual gauge. However during the inter-war years an improved road was constructed between the French border town of Briançon and Turin, which had a serious effect upon the fortunes of the line. As a result, this historic railway was closed in 1968 in favour of the local bus service which was able to provide the transport needs of the community.

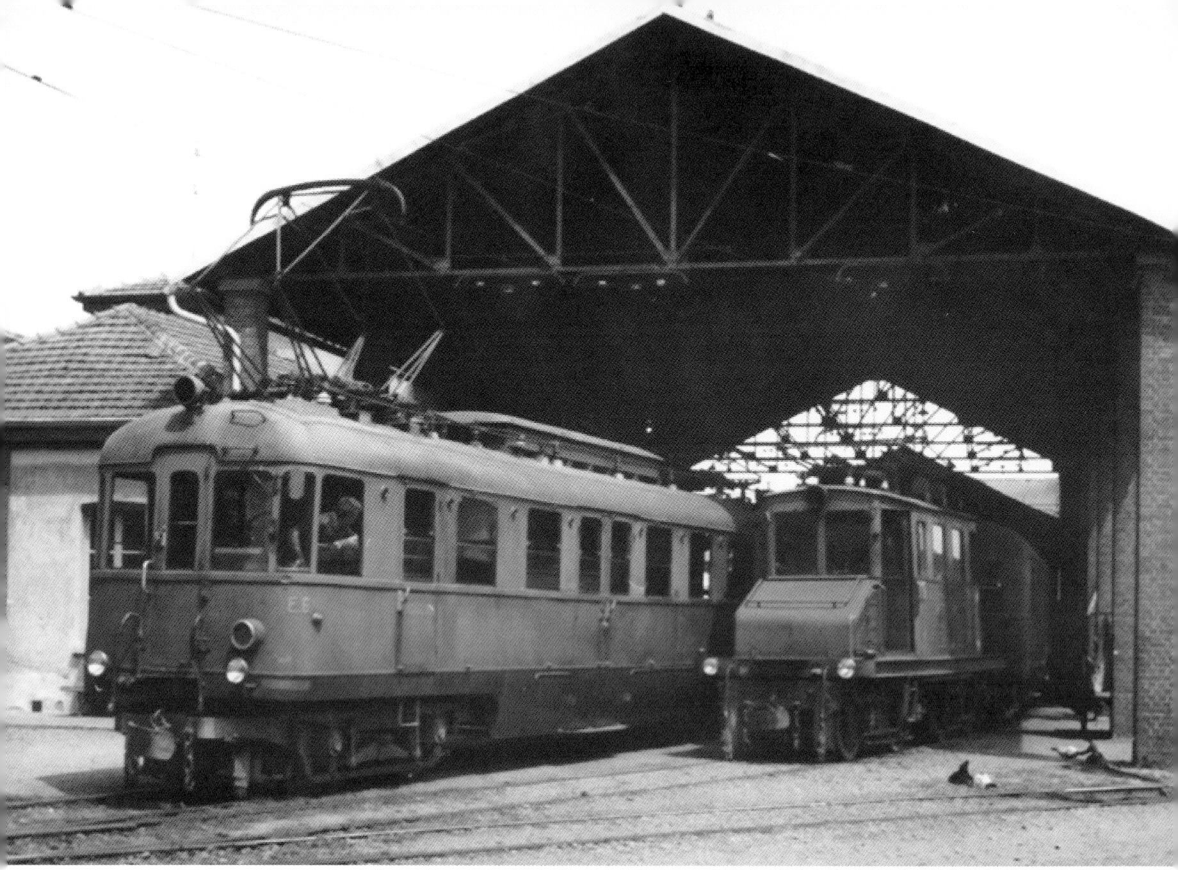

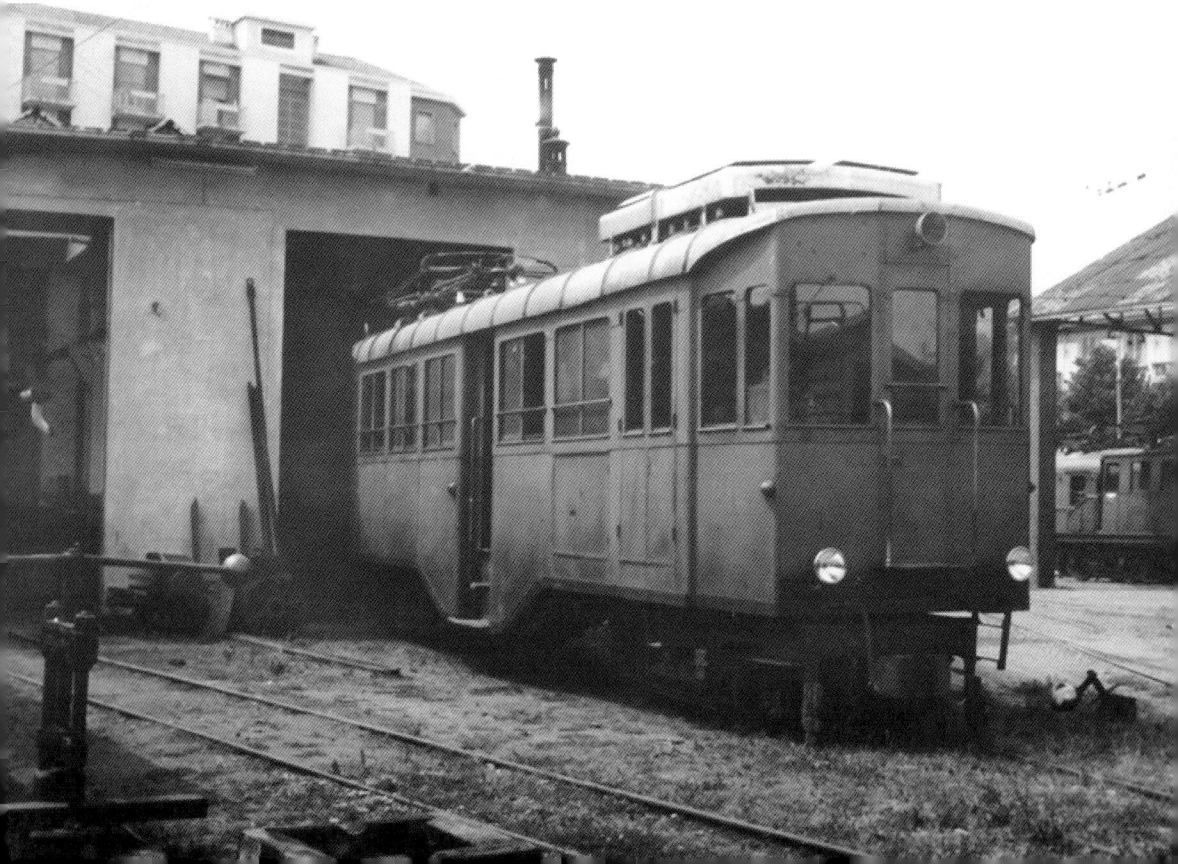

← 3.1.   The overall roof of the station at Pinerola provided the location for this view of two trains of the former Piedmont Steam Tramway. The electric locomotive on the right dates from the electrification of the route in 1928, this photograph being taken during the final period of operation on 6th August 1966. (J.Wiseman)

← 3.2.   Opposite the station was the depot of the line, where one of the 1100mm gauge electric railcars was also viewed on the same occasion. (J.Wiseman)

3.3.   The train seen in photograph 3.1 was witnessed as it passed through the main square at Pinerola during the first stage of its journey to Perosa on 6th August 1966. (J.Wiseman)

3.4. No.E2, one of the BoBo electric locomotives supplied in 1928, is seen alongside the roadside station at Villar Perosa on the same date. (J.Wiseman)

3.5. Shortly after the previous photograph was recorded, no.E2 prepares to leave Villar Perosa whilst hauling a train bound for Pinerola. The roadside nature of the route can be fully appreciated in this scene. (J.Wiseman)

FERROVIA GENOA – CASELLA

The important port of Genoa (Genova) is surrounded by mountainous terrain, particularly to the north. Although a main line connection existed between Genoa and both Turin and Milan, some of the mountain communities were devoid of transport until 1929. In that year a metre gauge railway, 24km in length, was constructed between Genoa Piazza Manin and Casella Paese.

This very scenic line incorporating many fine viaducts with an average gradient of 1 in 22 was electrified from the outset with a 2400 volt DC overhead system. The line has continued to serve the mountain communities with an invaluable service until the present time. Although some of the original stock has survived, these have been supplemented by material inherited from lines that have succumbed to closure during the last 40 years or so. The scenic attributes of this line alone should secure its future and is a highly recommended inclusion to any itinerary for a visit to this part of Italy.

VI. The mountainous route of this line, as it climbs in a northward direction from Genoa Piazza Manin, is shown in this diagram of the area. (BVA)

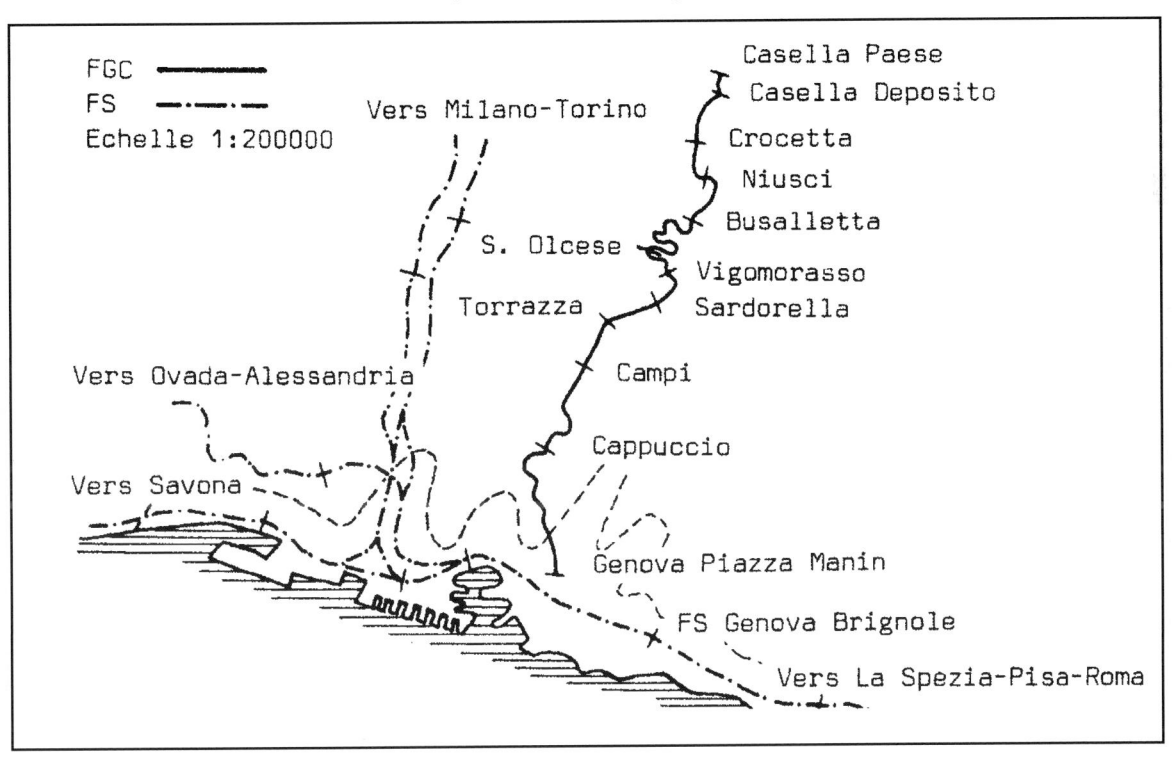

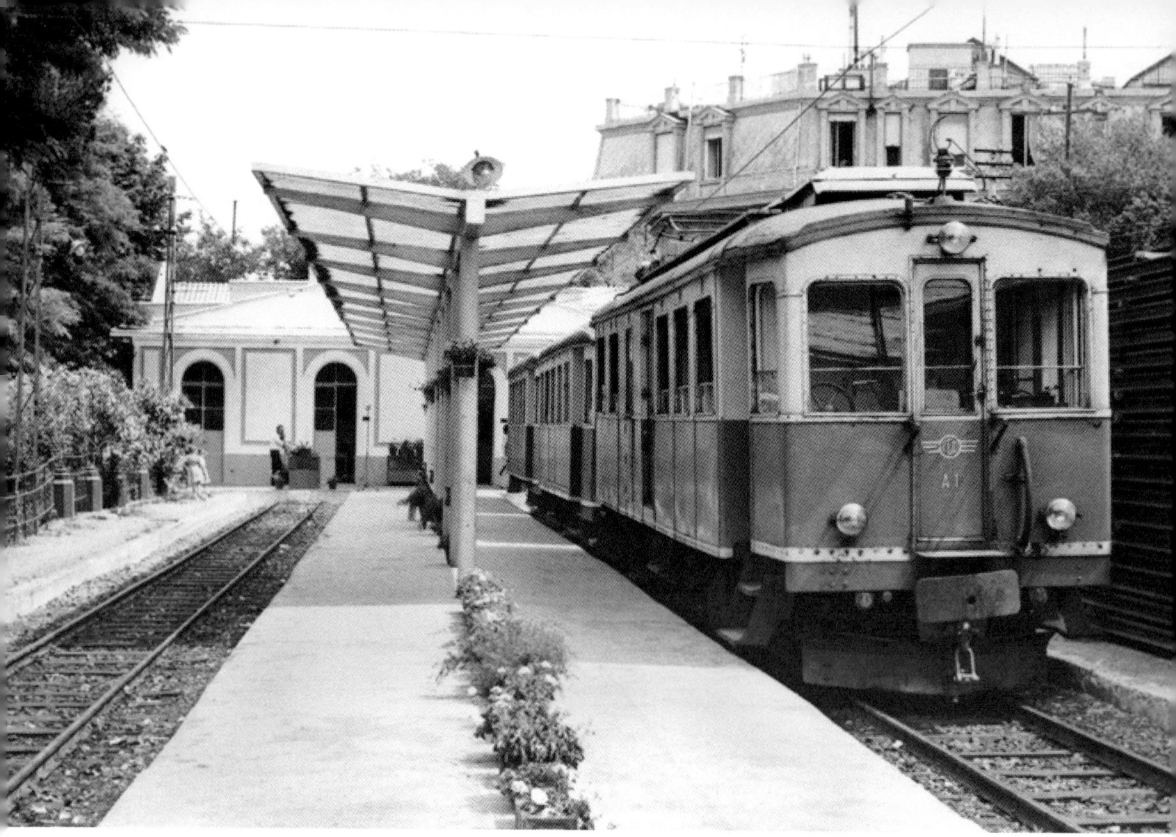
A1

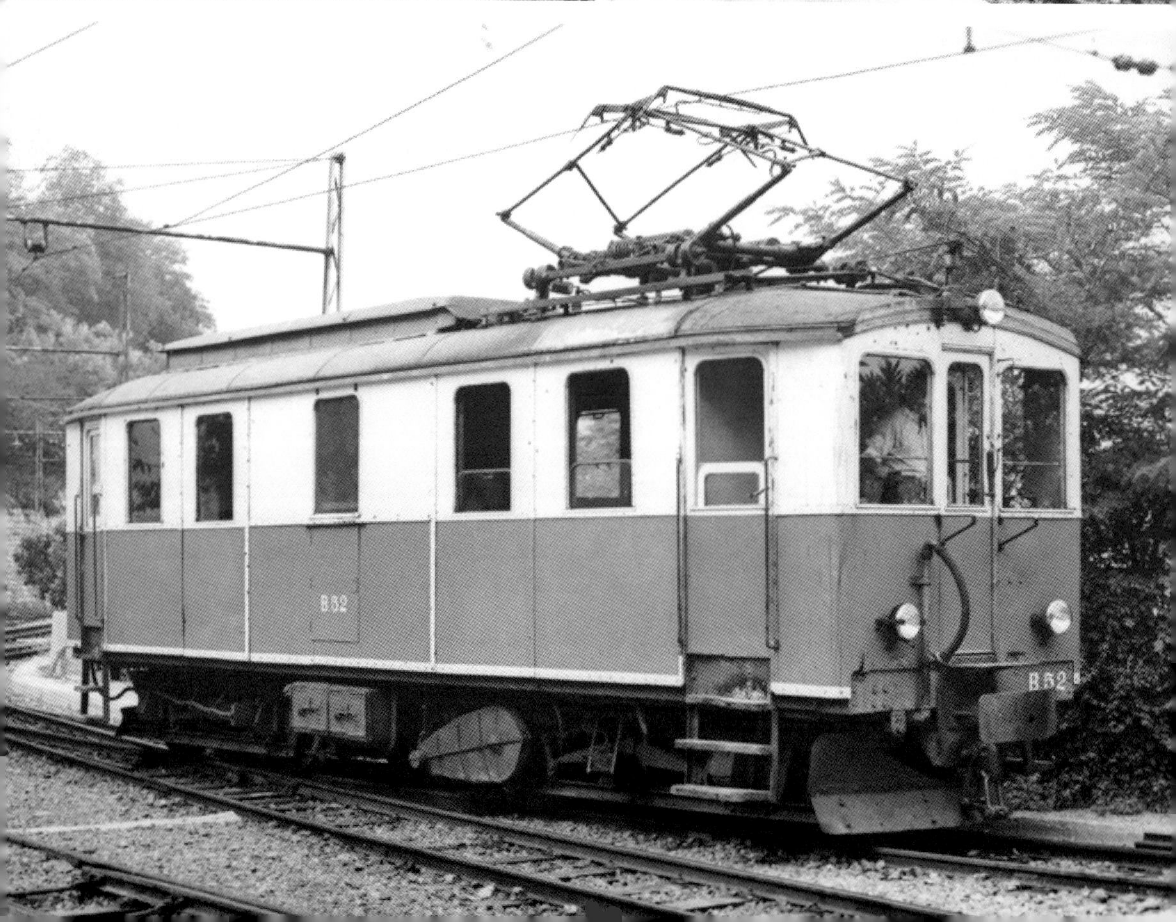
B 52
B 52

← 3.6.   The delightful station of Genoa Piazza Manin features in this view of railmotor no.A1 at the head of a train, shortly prior to departure for Casella on 11th July 1976. (H.Rohrer /BVA)

← 3.7.   On the same occasion, railmotor no. B52 was recorded as it approached the station at Genoa Piazza Manin. (H.Rohrer /BVA)

3.8.   During the initial ascent from Genoa, a Casella bound mixed train was witnessed as it crossed the viaduct at Cappuccio on 5th August 1978. (H.Rohrer /BVA)

3.9. The viaduct at Cappuccio can be seen it the background in this view of no.B52 descending towards Genoa with a freight train on 10th July 1976. (H.Rohrer /BVA)

➔ 3.10. At the midway station situated at Vigomorasso, a Casella bound train hauled by no.A1 passes former Spoleto-Norcia unit no.A4 on 10th July 1976. (H.Rohrer /BVA)

➔ 3.11. High in the mountains at S.Olcese-Chiesa, no.A6 was viewed during the ascent towards Casella on 5th August 1978. Like no.A4 seen in the previous photograph, this electric railcar was obtained from the Spoleto-Norcia line in 1968. (H.Rohrer /BVA)

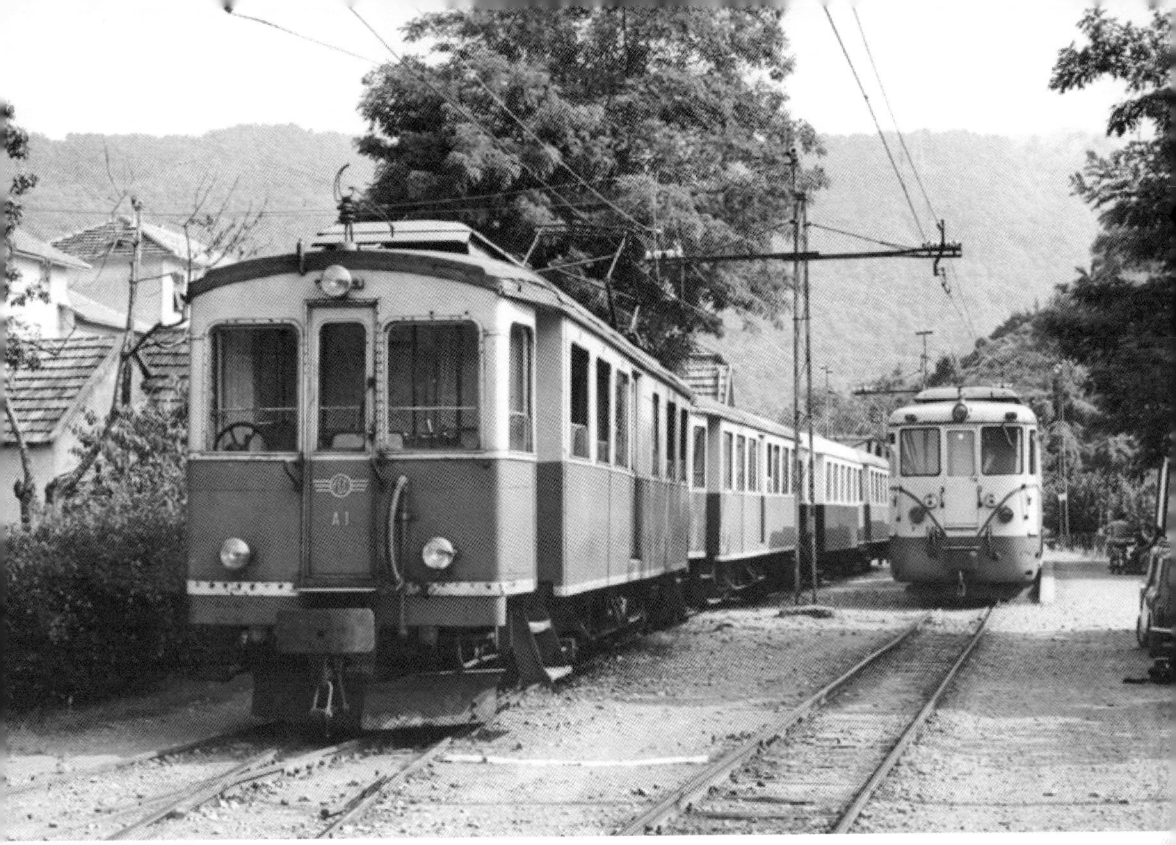
A 1

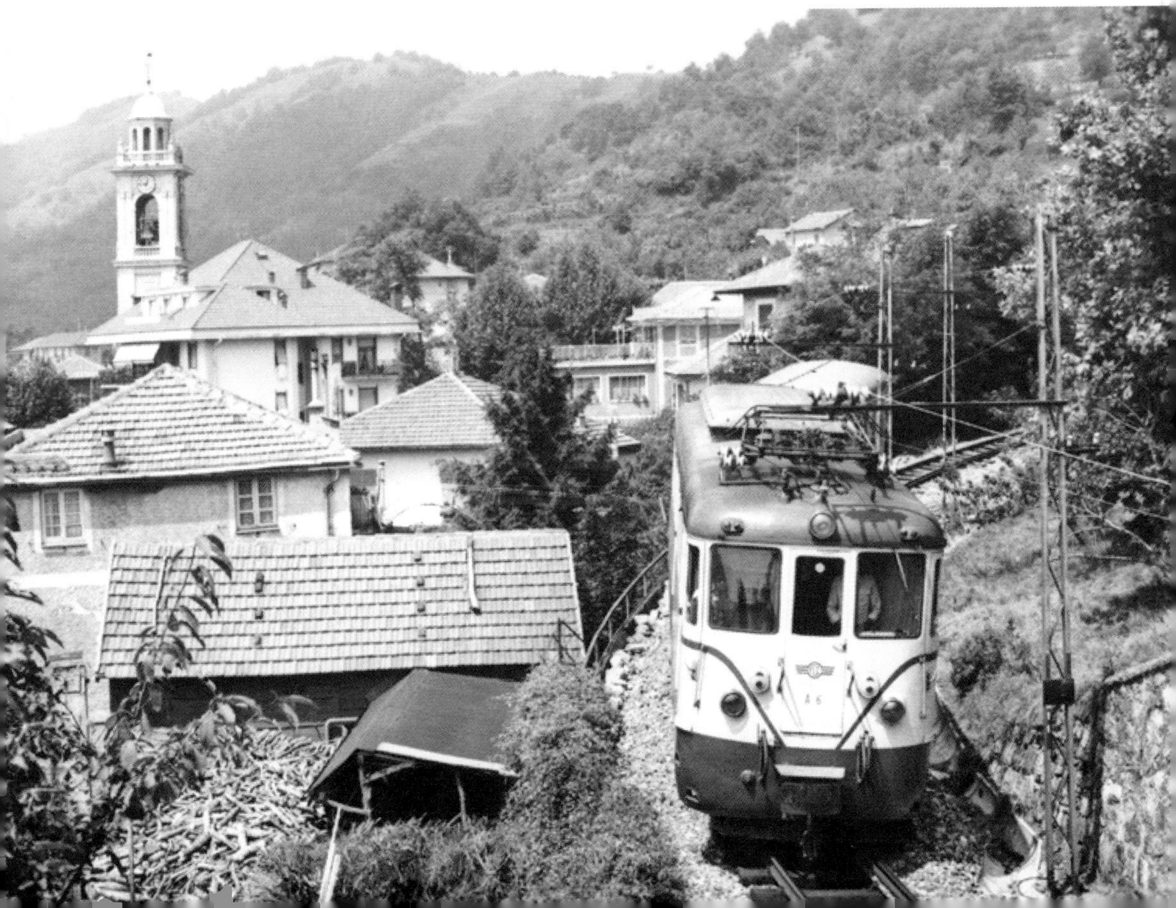
A 6

3.12. Three stages of the sinuous route above S.Olcese can be seen in this picture of a freight train climbing towards Casella on the same date. (H.Rohrer /BVA)

➔ 3.13. Nos A4 and A5 were recorded on the higher reaches of the route, as they passed at Busalletta on 5th August 1978. (H.Rohrer /BVA)

➔ 3.14. No.29, one of the earlier generation of tramcars, was recorded at Crocetta on 10th July 1976. (H.Rohrer /BVA)

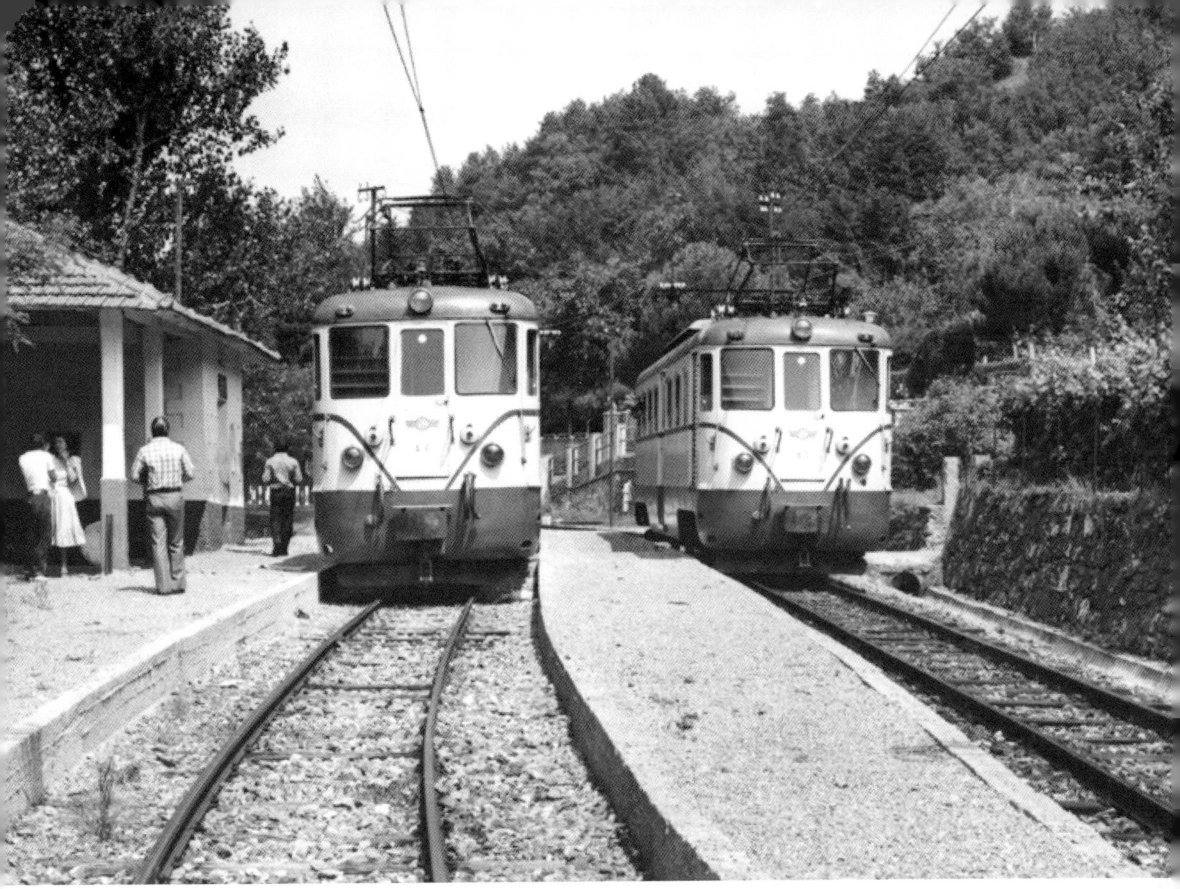

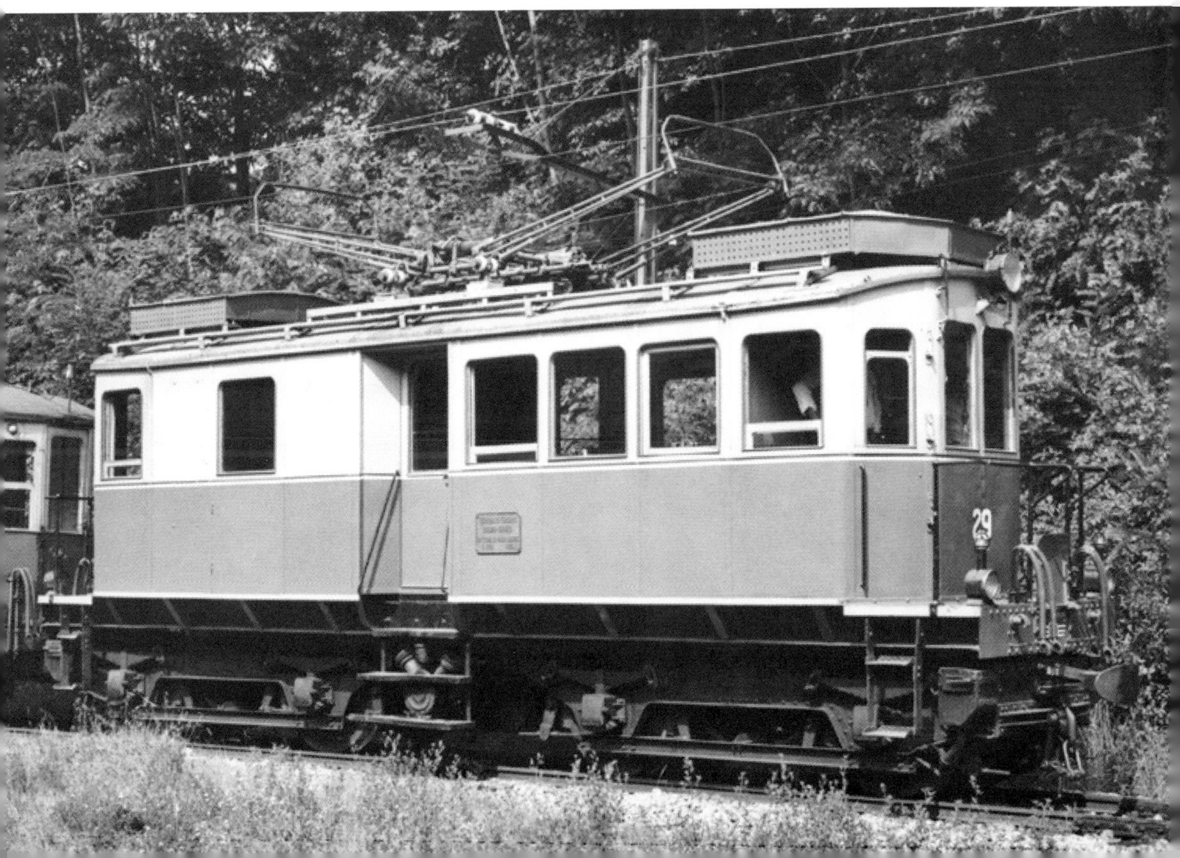
29

3.15. On the final approach to Casella, a train hauled by one of the older locomotives is seen as it crossed the viaduct at Deposito on the same occasion. (H.Rohrer /BVA)

➔ 3.16. A closer view of the same viaduct, but from a different angle, features in this scene of a single unit crossing the structure during the final part of its journey from Genoa on 5th August 1978. (H.Rohrer /BVA)

➔ 3.17. The upper terminus at Casella-Paese was recorded in this view of no.A2 at the roadside station on 10th July 1976. (H.Rohrer /BVA)

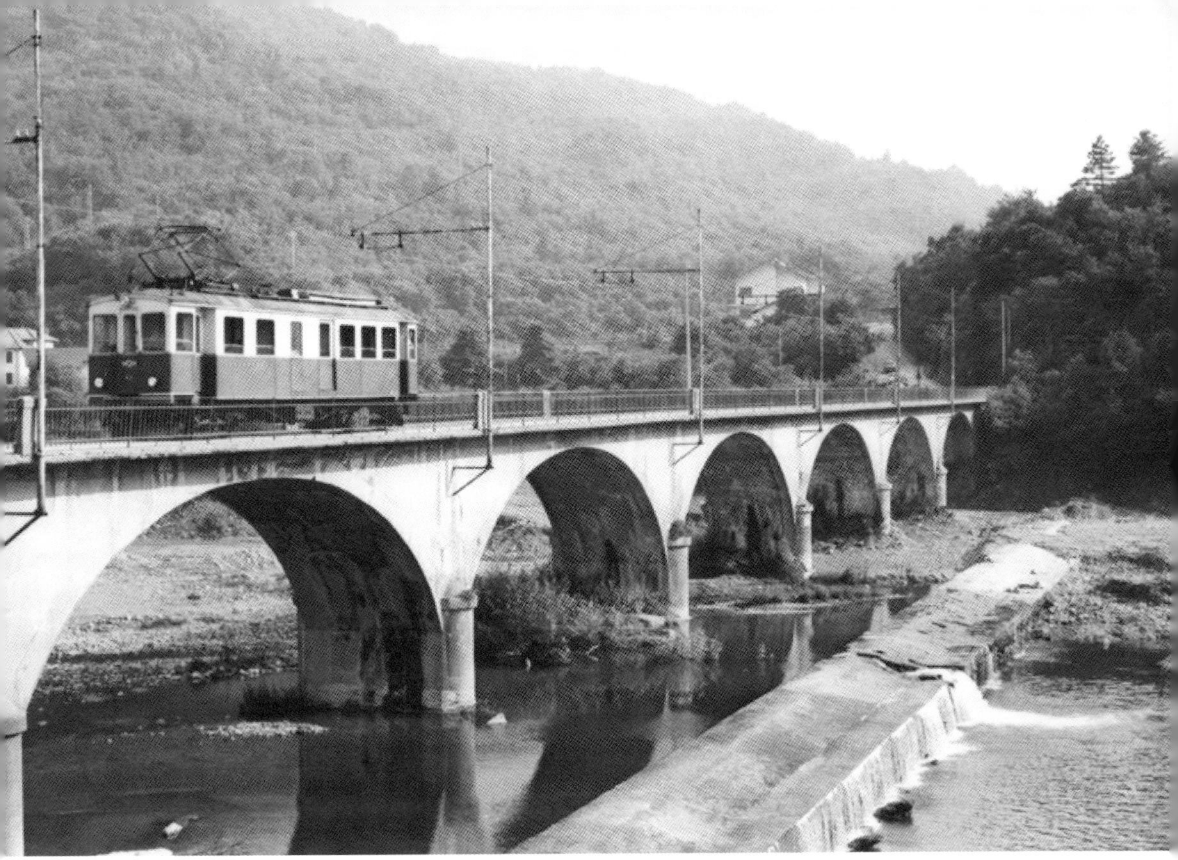

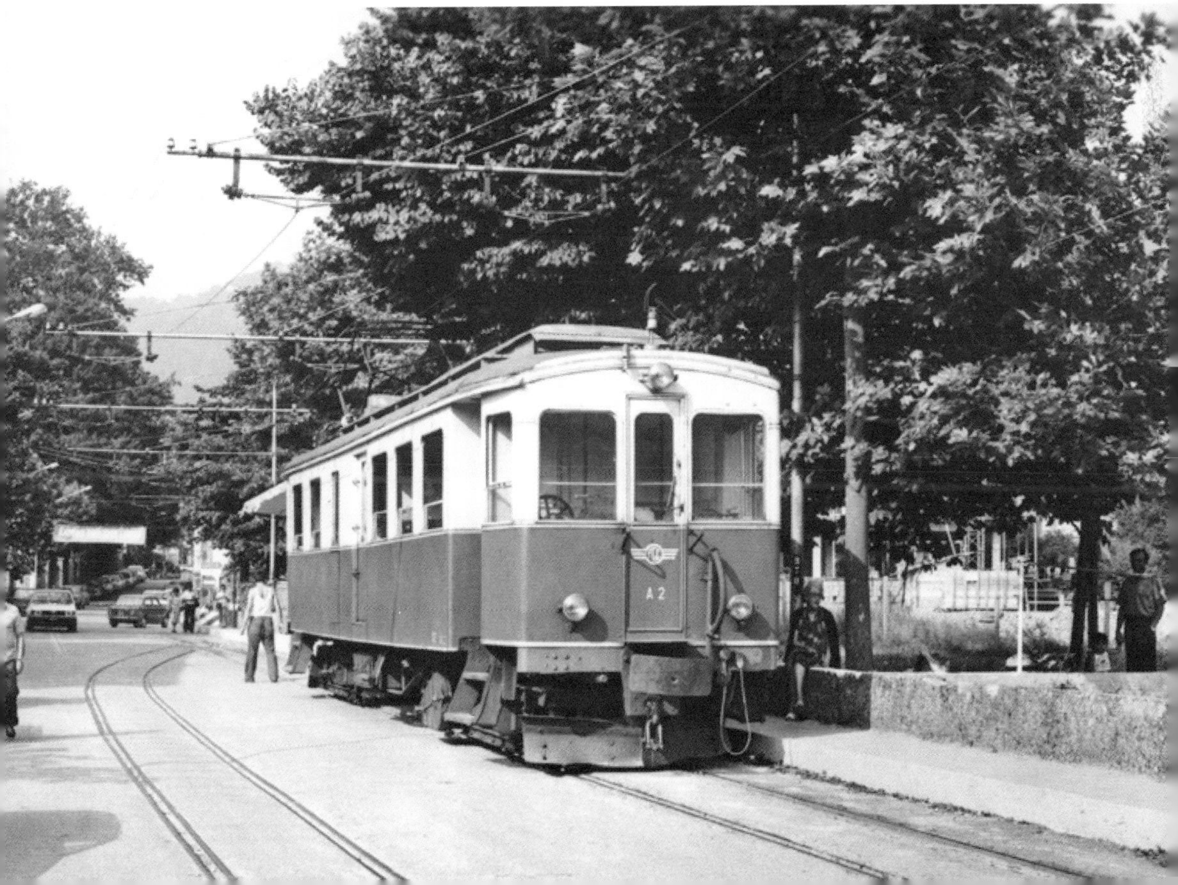
A 2

4. The Adriatic Coast and Umbria

The coastal area of the Adriatic Sea between Venice and Pescara has in recent years become a popular holiday destination, with its vast sandy beaches to rival those on the Mediterranean. Likewise the mountainous region of Umbria in the Appennines has now developed a tourist industry throughout the year. Sadly, the interesting narrow gauge railways that once traversed this eastern part of Italy have all succumbed to modernisation, although one has been adapted as a scenic long distance footpath.

FERROVIA RIMINI-NOVAFELTRIA

To the west of the coastal resort of Rimini lies the independent state of San Marino. This enclave was once connected to the coast by a 950mm gauge railway, which passed along the northern border of San Marino. The line terminated on Italian soil at Novafeltria, 34km from Rimini. Construction of this railway commenced in 1916, but was not completed until 1922 as a result of the disruption caused by World War One.

Initially operated by steam locomotives, the original machines remained in use until 1952 when they were supplemented by three diesel railcars. The steam locomotives consisted of two Breda 0-8-0Ts, and an Orenstein & Koppel 0-6-0T. These were joined by a Krauss 0-4-0Tr tram locomotive dating from 1900, which was acquired secondhand in 1932 from a long extinct tramway that ran between Ferrara and Codigoro to the north of Bologna. The railcars were supplied by Ranieri of Rome and were powered by General Motors engines, based on the power units fitted to Sherman Tanks of WW2.

As with many other similar narrow gauge railways, an improved road network ultimately rendered the operation obsolete, the result being that the line closed in 1960. However some reminders of its past glory survived. The railcars were transferred to Sicily, where they were still at work until the recent past. The Krauss tram locomotive was ultimately sold to the Blonay-Chamby museum line in Switzerland in 1970 where, following re-gauging to metre gauge, it became one of the first working exhibits at that splendid operation near Montreux (see *Swiss Narrow Gauge*).

VII. The 950mm line from the coast to the foothills of the mountainous interior, passing close to San Marino, is depicted in this diagram.

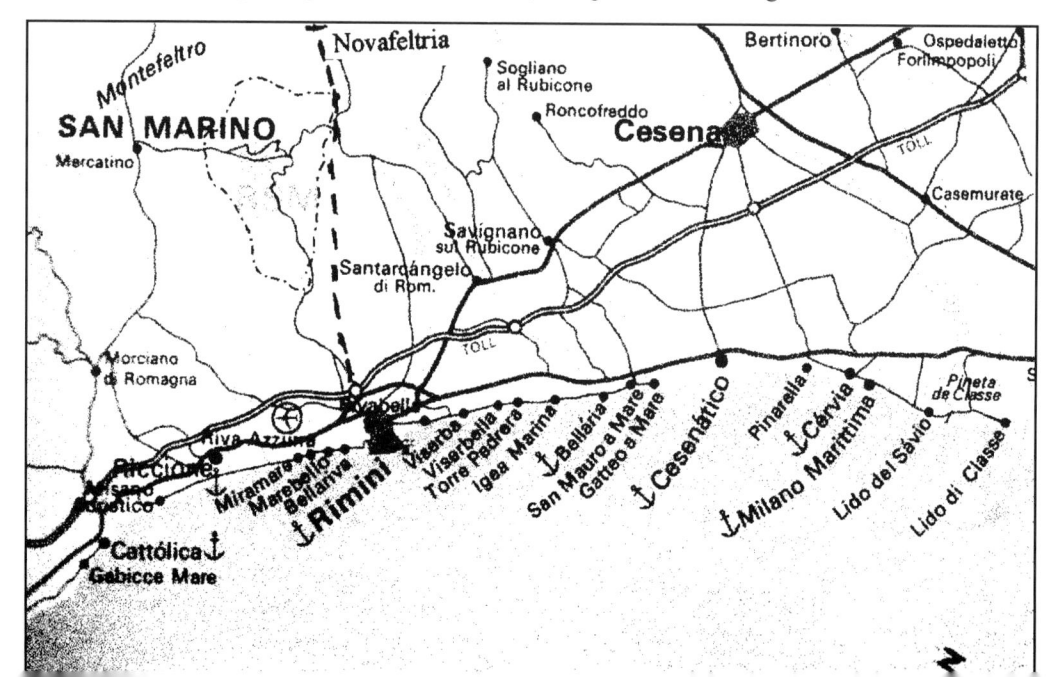

4.1. Shortly before the closure of the line, one of the Ranieri railcars was viewed at rest inside the two road depot at Rimini. One of the Breda 0-8-0Ts is also visible alongside the building in this scene recorded on 17th September 1959. (D.Trevor Rowe)

4.2. No.4, the Krauss 0-4-0Tr tram locomotive, survived to live another day. Following a period in store it was purchased by the Blonay-Chamby railway museum in 1970. The historic machine was seen inside the main exhibition hall at Chamby on 1st September 1990. (J.F.Organ)

PESCARA – PENNE

Further south along the Adriatic coast, the port of Pescara is the location of the ferry terminal that once provided a connection with the Croatian port of Split. During the last decade, this service has been transferred to Ancona, further north. However, Pescara is still an important port, being served by the FS route that traverses the east coast of Italy and also a cross country route to Rome. Of more interest to this publication is the fact that there once was an electrified 950mm gauge tramway that connected Pescara to Penne, 25km to the west. Penne is located in the foothills of the Appennine Mountains and has now become a popular tourist destination. Sadly, the tramway closed in 1963 and was not destined to feature in the developments of the area.

4.3.   A train from Penne is seen as it travelled along the main street of Pescara. The FS coastal route is beyond the fence to the left of this photograph from 2nd June 1963, shortly before the tramway closed. (J.Wiseman)

4.4.   The tramway terminated in the street outside the FS station, where electric railcar no.2 was viewed running round its carriages on the same occasion. (J.Wiseman)

4.5. A works train was recorded as it passed the grass strewn tracks leading to the depot, a short distance to the north of Pescara, on 3rd June 1963. (J.Wiseman)

4.6. At Montesilvemo, midway along the route of the roadside tramway, a two-car combination was photographed en-route from Penne on the same date. (J.Wiseman)

SPOLETO – NORCIA

The mountainous region of Umbria, in the centre of Italy, was until the early years of the 20th century, almost devoid of access to the main centres of commerce and industry. As part of the need to improve this situation, a 51km long electric tramway was constructed in 1926 to connect the town of Spoleto with Norcia, a smaller town situated high in the Appennines. This 950mm gauge line provided an important means of transport in the area until 1968, when an improved road network resulted in its closure.

The route has now been developed as a scenic long distance footpath, whilst the surviving tramcars were transferred to the Genoa to Casella line. These obviously required conversion to metre gauge before they could work at their new home.

4.7. The constricted terminus at Spoleto Cittá was the location for this view of no. A4 prior to its departure to Norcia on 26th May 1963. As noted in Section 3 of this publication, this vehicle was transferred to the Genoa-Caselle line following the closure of the Spoleto-Norcia route in 1968. (J.Wiseman)

4.8. One of the earlier electric motor units is seen outside the depot at Spoleto on the same occasion. (J.Wiseman)

4.9. A selection of rolling stock was also recorded in the sidings alongside the depot at Spoleto Cittá on 26th May 1963. (J.Wiseman)

4.10. No.A2 was witnessed as it paused at Sant'Anatolia during the course of a journey from Spoleto to Norcia on the same date. (J.Wiseman)

4.11. Car no.A2 was recorded as it climbed away from Sant'Anatolia whilst on the same journey of 26th May 1963. (J.Wiseman)

5. Rome and Naples

The area in the vicinity of the nation's capital of Rome possessed only one narrow gauge railway of note, the last remnants of which remain as part of the city urban transport network. By contrast, the coastal city of Naples and its immediate area were well endowed with an extensive network, the majority of which is still providing an invaluable service to the local community and extensive tourist industry in this part of Italy. With so many historical sites, combined with a coastline of extreme beauty, these surviving lines are guaranteed a continuing future.

FERROVIA ROMA-FIUGGI

Opened in 1916, following three years of construction work, the first section of this 950mm railway connected Rome with Fiuggi, to the south east of the capital. The following year two branches were opened from Fiuggi to serve outlying communities which resulted in a network 78km in length. The operating company was Società per le Ferrovie Vicinali (SFV) and from the outset the line was electrified on an 850volt DC system. The terminus of the SFV in Rome was situated immediately alongside the FS main line station.

During 1943-44, the line was partly destroyed by allied bombing, but was rebuilt and re-opened in 1945. The operation continued unchanged until 1982 when the lines around Fiuggi were closed. The route was further reduced in 1983 when the outer terminus was replaced by one at Pantano, 18kms from Rome. This continued until 2008 when the line was effectively closed, although the section within the confines of Rome was adapted as part of the city urban Metro system.

5.1. Some of the historic ruins of ancient Rome can be seen in this view of car no.817, as it passes through Roma Viale Giolitti whilst en-route to Fiuggi on 30th May 1963. (J.Wiseman)

5.2. In a rural location near Fiuggi, no.453 was recorded whilst working a local service from Fiuggi Fonte to Alatri on 2nd August 1962. (J.Wiseman)

5.3. The extensive terminus complex at Fiuggi Fonte was featured in this busy scene witnessed on 2nd August 1962. On the left of the photograph, no.803 was about to depart for Rome, whilst no.453 was working the local service shown in the previous view. (J.Wiseman)

FERROVIA ALIFANA

In 1913 the first section of a complex network of 950mm lines to the north of Naples was opened. The line was extended to Santa Maria Capua Vetere, 43km from Naples, in 1914 together with a branch line from Caiazzo to Piedimonte. With the exception of the Piedimonte line, the FA was electrified on an 11000volt AC system. The branch line initially relied on steam haulage.

The line suffered heavy damage during WW2 and was largely abandoned. Part of the route was rebuilt to standard gauge in 1963, whilst the remainder was officially closed in 1976. Some of the former route has been adapted to form part of the Naples Metro system, which has been under construction since 2005.

5.4. Ferrovia Alifana no.3 is seen as it reversed into the station at Santa Maria Capua Vetere on 1st October 1974. (J.Wiseman)

5.5. FA no.9 and a single carriage were witnessed upon arrival at the station on the same occasion. (J.Wiseman)

5.6. Car no.3 was recorded as it departed from Santa Maria Capua Vetre whilst en-route to Naples on 1st October 1974, during the final months of the Ferrovia Alifana operation in its original guise. (J.Wiseman)

CIRCUMVESUVIANA (SFSM)

As its name suggests, this extensive 950mm gauge railway encircles the infamous volcano of Mount Vesuvius, to the southeast of Naples. Operated by Strade Ferrate Secondarie Meridionali (SFSM), the route also serves the Sorrento peninsula to the south. This coastal line incorporates the route of the first railway in Italy, a short line from Naples to the royal palace at Portici, which was opened as early as 1839. The first section of what was to become the SFSM was completed in 1891 between Naples and Ottaviano, a distance of 23km. The original coastal route was rebuilt and electrified in 1905, with an extension to Pompei Scavi, which is located a short distance from the historic excavations.

During the inter-war years, the line was further extended until the network had a total length of 138km serving 96 stations by 1936. The entire route was electrified by that time, on a 1500volt DC system. Despite damage incurred during WW2, plus a serious eruption of Vesuvius in 1944, upgrading and modernization of the SFSM was resumed in 1948. Since that time much of the route has been rebuilt with a double track formation, whilst the motive power and rolling stock have been progressively upgraded.

The principal trains were formerly hauled by powerful 1-D-1 (2-8-2) electric locomotives, although the extensive local services were in the hands of two and three-car EMU sets. These have been progressively updated over the years, culminating in a fleet of 26 "Metrostar" three car units supplied jointly by Breda and Firema in 2009.

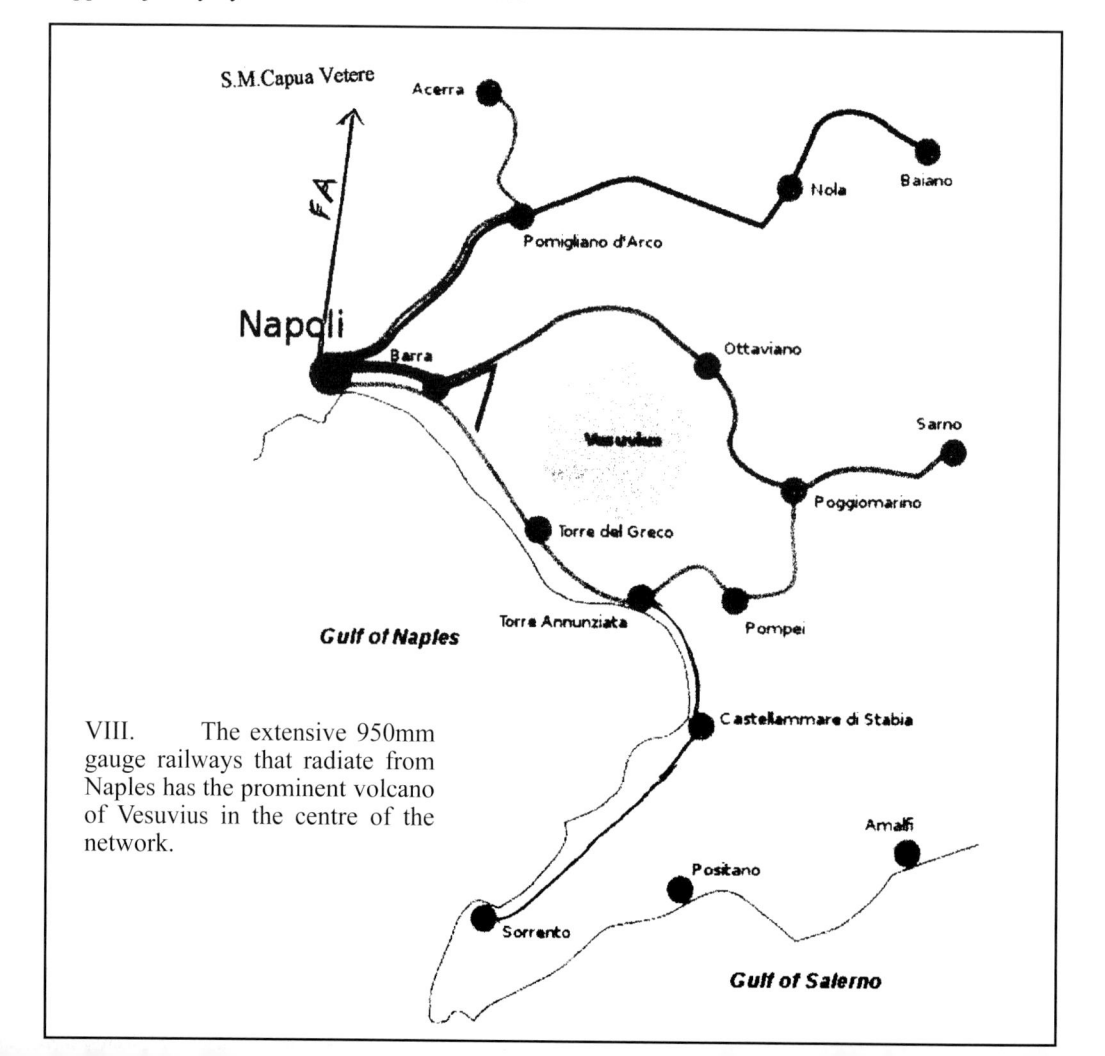

VIII. The extensive 950mm gauge railways that radiate from Naples has the prominent volcano of Vesuvius in the centre of the network.

5.7. The Naples terminus of the SFSM was the location of no.0201 at the head of a long train awaiting departure to Sorrento. A tram can be seen crossing the long bridge spanning the station complex in this scene recorded on 4th August 1962. (J.Wiseman)

5.8. No.0302, one of the impressive 1-D-1 electric locomotives, was viewed in the station at Naples on the same occasion. These powerful machines were used for hauling the principal trains on the SFSM for many years. (J.Wiseman)

5.9   A local train was recorded as it traversed the station avoiding line on 4th August 1962. (J.Wiseman)

5.10   A train from Pompei is pictured in the southern outskirts of Naples at Ercolano, during May 2007.   (P.Lawson)

5.11. With a backdrop of modern apartments, the same train departs from Ercolano towards Naples in May 2007. (P.Lawson)

6. Puglia and Calabria

The area that constitutes the "heel and toe" of Italy, which embraces the regions of Puglia and Calabria, possesses the largest concentration of narrow gauge railways in the country. Due to the difficult terrain that was encountered, the choice of gauge was dictated from the outset, 950mm being the preferred option in common with many other Italian lines. Apart from an independent 750mm line centred around the port of Bari, The extensive 950mm gauge routes were constructed over a long period between 1915 and 1956 by the Mediterraneo Calabro-Lucane (MCL), later to become Ferrovie Calabro-Lucane (FCL) which served Bari on the Adriatic coast, whilst to the south Cosenza, Catanzaro and Gioia Tauro were the principal termini. At its ultimate extent the system totalled 765km in length, the majority of which is still extant.

In 1991 the FCL was divided into two separate operations with the northern section based at Bari managed by the Ferrovie Appulo-Lucane (FAL) whilst the southern section under the management of the Ferrovie della Calabria (FdeC) was controlled from Catanzaro. More importantly the majority of the former FCL system has survived, only some little used lines in outlying areas having succumbed to closure during the 1970s.

IX. The inland route followed by the former tramway between the two coastal termini is clearly shown in this sketch. (P.C.Allen/P.B.Whitehouse)

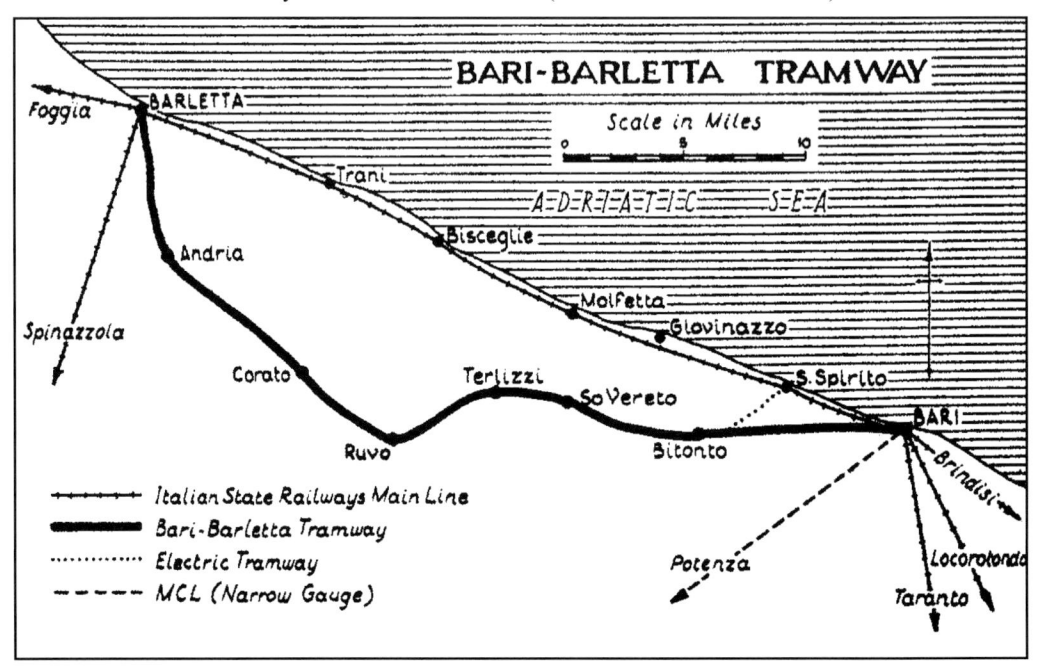

BARI – BARLETTA TRAMWAY

Constructed by the Belgian company Sociètè des Chemins de fer economics de Bari-Barletta SA, this 64 km long 750mm gauge line was opened in 1883. Built to connect the ports of Bari and Barletta on the Adriatic coast, the line took an inland route in order to serve the communities in the area. Ultimately the two ports were connected by the FS standard gauge route that runs along the entire length of the Italian coast. The original company was declared bankrupt in 1934, the tramway being transferred to the Ferrotramviaria SpA who continued to operate the line until it closed in 1959. However the route has survived as part of the FS network, which rebuilt the line to standard gauge during the 1960s and electrified it with a 3000 volt DC system, in common with the state system.

During its original form as a steam operated tramway, the motive power was principally provided by a fleet of 0-6-2Ts supplied by the Sociètè St. Léonard, Liège in 1881. During the ensuing years these were joined by a number of locomotives acquired secondhand including a former War Department Hunslet 4-6-0T, which would have required re-gauging from its original 600mm.

6.1. Shortly after the closure of the tramway, five of the Belgian built 0-6-2Ts were recorded at Bari awaiting their fate on 18th September 1959. (D.Trevor Rowe)

6.2. A more detailed view of St.Léonard 0-6-2T no.9 was obtained on the same occasion. The redundant carriages were stored on an adjacent siding. (D.Trevor Rowe)

FERROVIE APPULO-LUCANE (FAL)

Opened and operated by the MCL in 1915, the 30km line from Bari southwest to Matera in Puglia was the initial section of what ultimately was to become an extensive system covering much of southern Italy. During the early 1930s, this line was extended to Potenza and Aviglano in the neighbouring region of Basilicata. During the same period additional branches were opened to Laurenzana and Montalbano Jonico plus an isolated section between Atena and Marsio Nuovo. Plans to connect this isolated branch with the remainder of the 290km long FAL system were never realised.

Although the FAL relies on a fleet of railcars supplied at various periods since 1934, it was originally a steam hauled operation. The majority of trains were hauled by a fleet of twenty-one 400 Class 2-6-0Ts built by CEMSA between 1930 and 1932. These powerful locomotives were fitted with Caprotti valve gear and were more than adequate for the duties for which they were assigned. Six of these Italian built locomotives have survived, three of them as static exhibits at various locations throughout the area. Of the other three, nos 402 and 421, were retained in working order for use on tourist and enthusiast trains between 1989 and 1997, when they were withdrawn in need of major boiler work.

6.3. One of the FCL Breda railcars, no.Mz204 was viewed as it crossed a rocky embankment to the North-East of Matera on 21st February 1974. (J.Wiseman)

6.4. Breda 0-8-0T no.357 was witnessed amid the extensive plethora of tracks at Matera, whilst a two-car DMU waits in the distance on the same date. (J.Wiseman)

6.5. Railcar no.M2DE54, supplied by Piaggio in 1937, was displaying its characteristic Italian lines when it was photographed at Matera on 27th September 1974. (J.Wiseman)

6.6. No.357 was recorded as it approached Matera whilst hauling a lightweight mixed train from Bari on 21st February 1974. (J.Wiseman)

6.7. CEMSA 2-6-0T no.418 was leaving Matera with a mixed train bound for Ferrandina, when it was also photographed on 21st February 1974. (J.Wiseman)

6.8. The same Italian built locomotive is seen upon arrival at Ferrandina on the same occasion in 1974. (J.Wiseman)

6.9. Following some shunting manoeuvres, no.418 was witnessed as it departed from Ferrandina with the return working to Matera later during the same day. (J.Wiseman)

6.10. The railcar depot at Potenza features in this view of a variety of period vehicles, including a rubber tyred interloper, on 23rd September 1959. (D.Trevor Rowe)

FERROVIE della CALABRIA (FdeC)

X. The extensive FCL network in the south of Italy, incorporating the current lines of the FAL and FdeC is shown in this diagram, which also includes projected extensions that were never achieved.

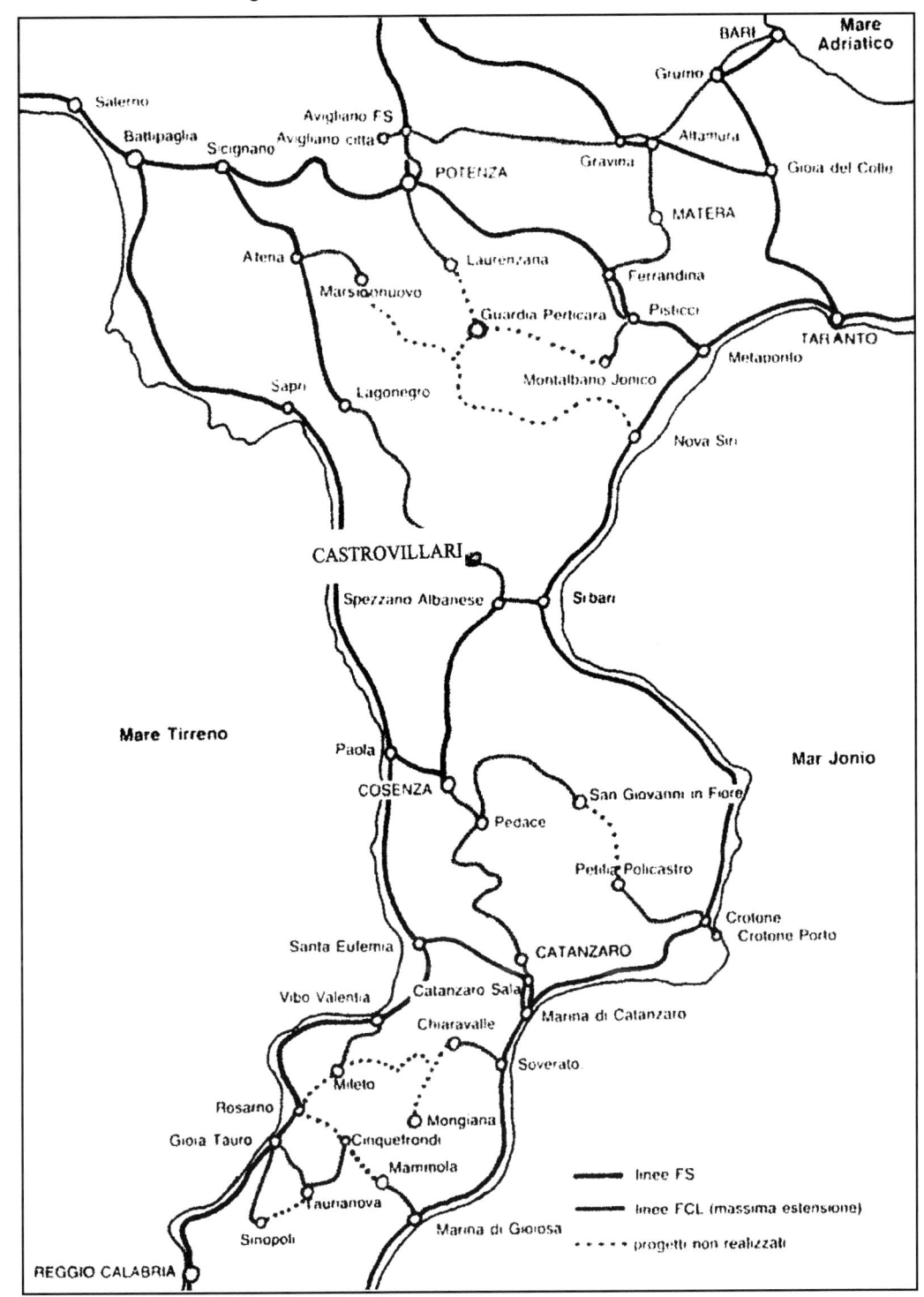

The first part of the southern section of the former MCL network was also opened in 1915, when the line linking Lagonegro to Spezzano Albanese Terme began operations in September of that year. This line, which included an Abt system rack section near Castrovillari, was destined to remain an isolated section connected to the FS system at each end of its route, until the rack section closed in 1971. In 1916 the first stage of the narrow gauge line to the south of Cosenza was opened, which ultimately extended to the Mediterranean coast at the hill-top city of Catanzaro. The final 2km link between Catanzaro Citta and Catanzaro Lido, which included another Abt system rack section, was completed in 1934.

    In 1922 a junction was created at Pedace, to the south of Cosenza, from where a spectacular steeply graded branch was constructed into the Sila Mountains. Initially terminating at San Pietro, it was extended to Camigliatello Silano in 1931 and this included gradients of 1 in 18. As late as 1956, this line was extended a further 27km through the mountains to San Giovanni in Fiore, the summit of the line being at San Nicola-Silvana Mansio at a height of 1406m. There were plans to extend this line to Petilia Policastro in order to connect with another FCL branch from Crotone. This proposal was not achieved, the Crotone branch being closed in 1970.

    Meanwhile another isolated section in the far south of Calabria was opened from Gioia Tauro along the coast to Sinopoli in 1917, with the remainder of the lines in the "toe of Italy" linking Gioia Tauro to Taurianova and Cinquefrondi being completed by 1929.

    Motive power on the former FCL section of the FdeC was largely in the hands of eleven powerful 0-8-0Ts of the 350 Class, which were originally supplied by Borsig in 1926. Later locomotives of the same class were built by both Breda and Ansoldo, the Italian machines being virtually identical to the Borsig's apart from being fitted with Caprotti valve gear in place of the Walschaerts equipment used on the German locomotives. For the rack and pinion sections of line, CEMSA supplied six 2-6-2RT locomotives in 1931 for which much technical assistance was supplied from Switzerland by SLM. As a consequence, these impressive locomotives bear a marked similarity to the 0-8-0RT and 0-8-2RT machines supplied by SLM for use in India and Indo-China (now Vietnam) during the 1920s. The lines radiating from Gioia Tauro were largely worked by a fleet of 2-6-0Ts of the 270 class, eighteen of which were supplied by Breda from 1923. These were subsequently augmented with some of the CEMSA 2-6-0Ts from the FAL section of the FCL.

    The FCL was a pioneer in the use of railcars, the first of which were supplied by Officine Meccaniche (OM) of Milan in 1934, whilst diesel powered locomotives eventually arrived on the scene in 1974, with the arrival of nine Bo-Bo diesel hydraulics of the 600 class supplied by both Breda and Ferrosud, some of which were ultimately transferred to the FAL section. However, the majority of services are operated with railcars, the majority of which were built by Breda between 1964 and 1984. The latest arrivals include twin-car units supplied by Stadler in 2009. Five of these DMU sets are rack fitted for use on the Abt section at Catanzaro.

    Surviving steam locomotives include Borsig 0-8-0T no.353 and CEMSA 2-6-2RTs nos 502,503,504 and 506. Whilst nos 503 and 506 are preserved as static exhibits in the area, the others are still officially retained as part of the FdeC stock. Between 1991 and 2008 no.353 was used on weekend excursions through the mountains between Camigliatello Silano and San Nicola-Silvana Mansio. It was finally retired at the expiry of its boiler certificate and has since remained in store at Cosenza. Also in store at Cosenza is no.504, which received a general overhaul in 2003. No.502 is in store near Catanzaro with the intention of it being returned to working order. Preserved on a plinth at Gioia Tauro is no.188, the last survivor of the Breda 270 Class 2-6-0Ts.

LAGONEGRO to SPEZZANO ALBANESE

6.11. This impressive viaduct at Lagonegro suffered serious storm damage during 1959, resulting in the temporary closure of this isolated section of the FCL system. The damaged structure is seen on 22nd September 1959. (D.Trevor Rowe)

6.12. The depot of this isolated section was a Castrovillari, where the locomotives used for the rack and pinion section to Spezzano Albanese were based. CEMSA 2-6-2RT no.503 was recorded outside the depot on 2nd November 1970. (J.Wiseman)

6.13. The SLM influence in the design of the locomotive as apparent in this view of no.503. Following the closure of the rack and pinion section in 1971, the rack fitted locomotives based at Castrovillari were transferred to Catanzaro. (J.Wiseman)

➜ 6.14. Prior to the introduction of the CEMSA 2-6-2RTs in 1931, the rack sections were the province of SLM 0-6-0RT locomotives, some of which ultimately worked in Sicily. A derelict no.262 was recorded at Castrovillari on 22nd September 1959. (D.Trevor Rowe)

➜ 6.15. Following the closure of the rack and pinion section, the surviving northern section of the Castrovillari line was worked by conventional locomotives. Breda 0-8-0T no.358 was viewed at the depot on 29th September 1974. (J.Wiseman)

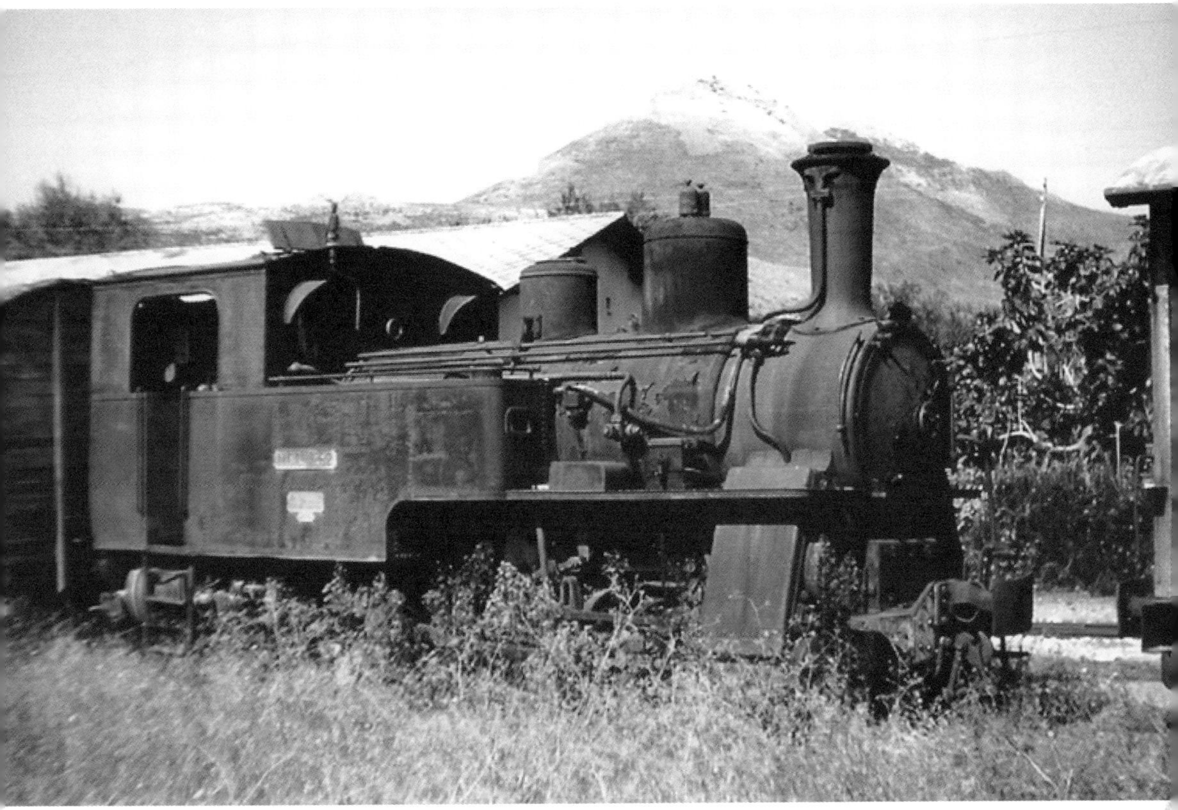

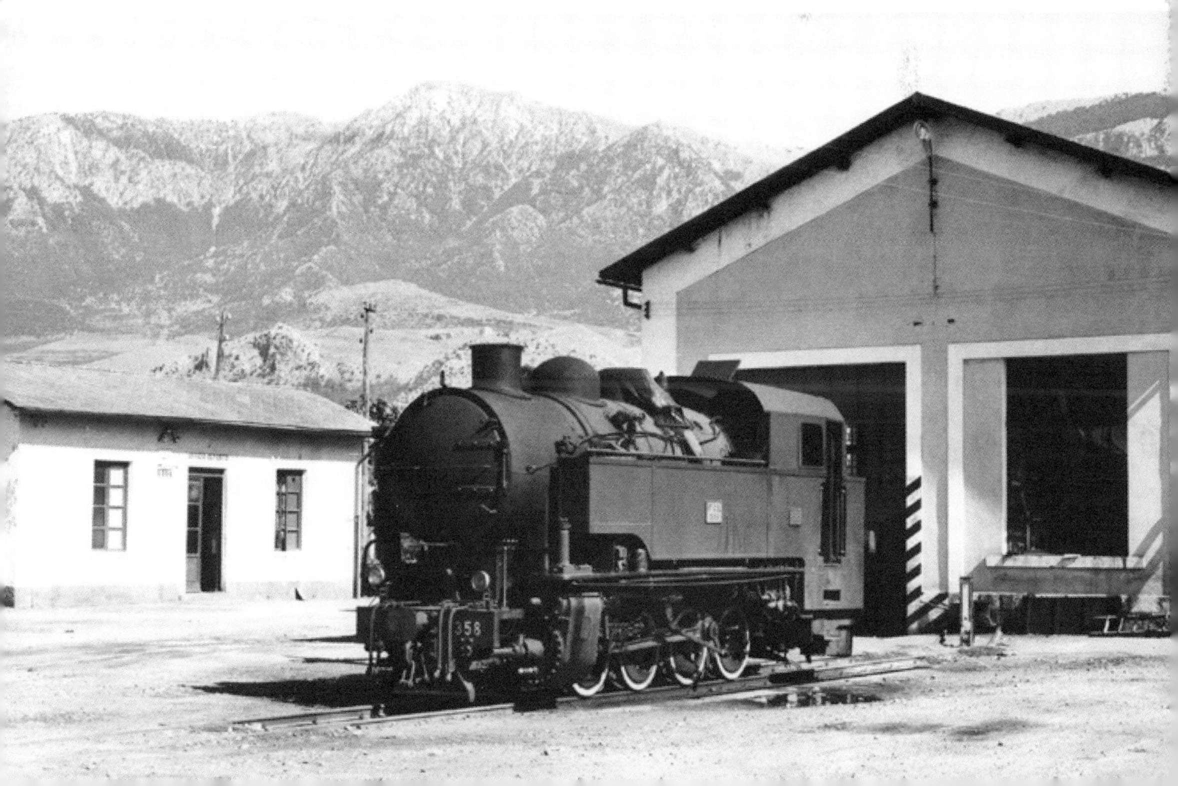
358

6.16. A rack fitted Ranieri railcar was photographed as it arrived at Spezzano Albanese on 22nd September 1959. (D.Trevor Rowe)

6.17. No.M1C81R, another of the Ranieri rack fitted railcars, was recorded at Spezzano Albanese on 2nd November 1970. (J.Wiseman)

COSENZA to SAN GIOVANNI IN FIORE

6.18. The fact that the FCL and its successors are responsible for all forms of public transport in the region is clearly shown in this view of Cosenza depot, with two buses astride the rails alongside 2-6-0T no. 417 on 21st September 1959. (D.Trevor Rowe)

6.19. Despite its location in the far south of Italy, snow is not unknown in the region served by the FdeC. Ansoldo 0-8-0T no.361 was fitted with a small snow plough when it was recorded at Cosenza on 31st October 1970. (J.Wiseman)

6.20. One of the surviving CEMSA 2-6-2RTs, no.504 was photographed outside the works at Cosenza in May 2006, having recently received a major overhaul. (P.Lawson)

6.21. With its rear pony truck removed, no.504 was viewed inside the immaculate and well equipped workshop at Cosenza during May 2007. (P.Lawson)

6.22. Borsig 0-8-0T no.353 is seen as it approached Cosenza from the south, whilst hauling a works train on 19th February 1974. (J.Wiseman)

6.23. Another view of the works train at the same location also shows some of the terrain which the FdeC section of the former FCL traverses. (J.Wiseman)

6.24. No.353 is pictured as it replenished its water supply at Rogliano, whilst hauling a freight train from Cosenza to Catanzaro on 30th September 1974. (J.Wiseman)

6.25.   Breda Bo-Bo diesel hydraulic locomotive no.606 was on shunting duties at Camigliatello Silano, whilst 0-8-0T no.353 was raising steam outside the shed in the background, when this scene was recorded during May 2007.   (P.Lawson)

6.26.   The impressive bulk of no.606 is apparent in this view of the locomotive with the stock of a tourist train that will be hauled by the steam locomotive through the mountains on the same occasion.   (P.Lawson)

6.27. Borsig 0-8-0T no.353 was the rostered steam locomotive, which was recorded as it departed from its shed towards the station and its waiting carriages. (P.Lawson)

6.28. Having coupled to its train, the German built 0-8-0T was about to depart from Camigliatello Silano with the tourist service to the summit of the line at San Nicola – Silvana Mansio in May 2007. (P.Lawson)

6.29. At an altitude of 1406m, San Nicola-Silvana Mansio is the highest station in Italy. No.353 was photographed following its arrival with the tourist train on the same occasion during 2007. (P.Lawson)

6.30. Opened as late as 1956, the terminus of the Sila branch line was located at San Giovanni in Fiore, where a Breda railcar was recorded alongside a pair of freight vans on 16th October 1995. (A.Heywood)

CATANZARO and CROTONE

6.31. The extensive depot at Catanzaro Citta features in this view of 2-6-2RT no.506 and an early Breda railcar on 20th September 1959.
(D.Trevor Rowe)

6.32. Rack fitted Ranieri railcar no. M1C84R was also photographed at Catanzaro Citta on the same occasion.
(D.Trevor Rowe)

6.33. A more recent view of Catanzaro Citta features three of the later Breda railcars at the station on 16th October 1995. The railcar at the rear was probably rack fitted for use on the Abt section to Catanzaro Lido. (A.Heywood)

6.34. Two of the Breda rack and pinion fitted railcars were recorded at the lower terminus at Catanzaro Lido during February 1994. (A.Heywood)

6.35. The isolated branch from Crotone to Petilia Policastro closed in 1970. Shortly after the closure, Breda 2-6-0T no.187 and Piaggio railcar trailer no. 89 were viewed at Crotone depot on 1st November 1970.   (J.Wiseman)

6.36. With a derelict works trolley in the foreground, no.187 was awaiting removal from Crotone for service elsewhere on the FCL network on the same date. (J.Wiseman)

6.37. No.M1 34, one of the Ranieri railcars rebuilt as a parcels van, was also in store at Crotone in November 1970. (J.Wiseman)

GIOIA TAURO – SINOPOLI – TAURIANOVA - CINQUEFRONDI

6.38. Ansoldo 0-8-0T no.361 and a 4w railcar were witnessed at Gioia Tauro on the southern section of the FCL (FdeC) system on 18th February 1974. (J.Wiseman)

6.39. No.361 was hauling a freight train from Cinquefrondi when it was recorded arriving at Gioia Tauro on 12th May 1975. (J.Wiseman)

6.40. The line from Gioia Tauro to Sinopoli is the most southern section of the FdeC. A railcar was viewed crossing this large steel girder viaduct near Gioia Tauro, with the FS line to Reggio di Calabria in the background, on 18th February 1974. (J.Wiseman)

6.41. In the "toe of Italy", Breda bogie railcar no.Mz75 is seen at Sinopoli basking in the winter sunshine on the same occasion. (J.Wiseman)

6.42. CEMSA 2-6-0T no.411 was also viewed at Sinopolo as it awaited departure with a freight train bound for Gioia Tauro on 18th February 1974. (J.Wiseman)

6.43.   0-8-0T no.361 is pictured shunting the stock of a freight train at Taurianova on 12th May 1975.   (J.Wiseman)

6.44.   The Italian built 0-8-0T also features in this view recorded at Taurianova on the same occasion.   (J.Wiseman)

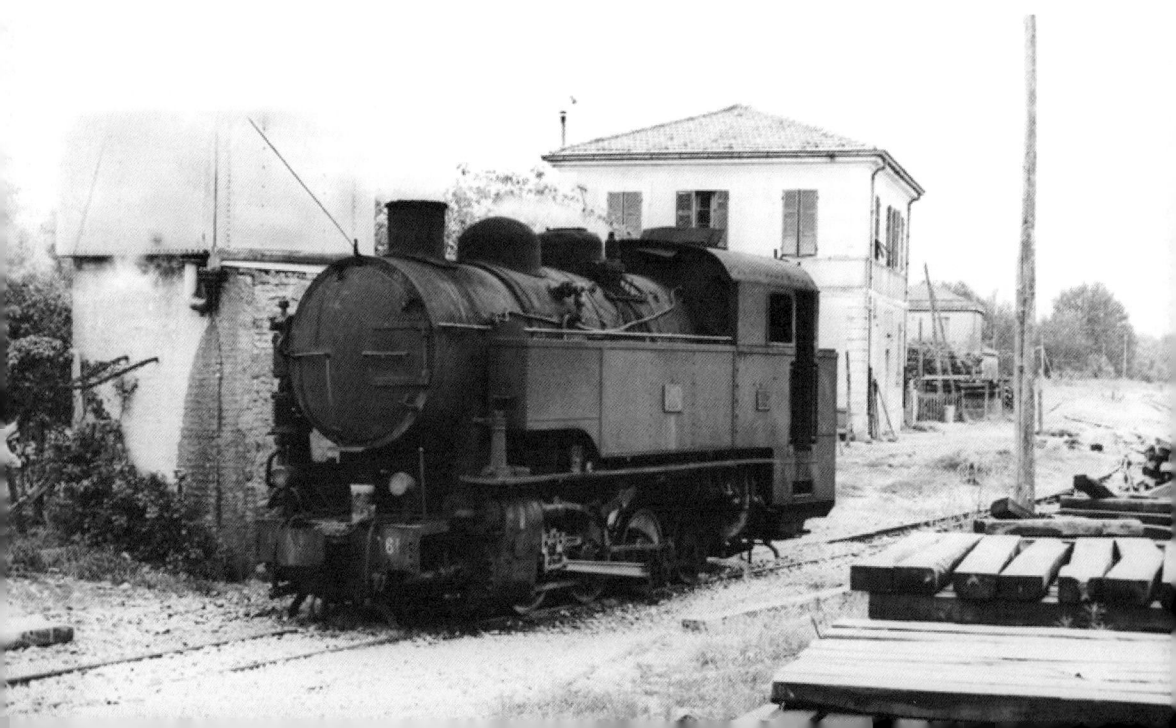

6.45.   Near to Cinquefrondi, the line from Taurianova crosses this masonary viaduct where a Breda railcar was recorded on 12th May 1975.   (J.Wiseman)

6.46. The same viaduct features in this view of 0-8-0T no.361 as it hauled a lightweight train across the structure on the same date. (J.Wiseman)

6.47. The Italian built locomotive of 1928 vintage was photographed at Cinquefrondi at the head of its lightweight train, with the delightful scenery of southern Italy as a backdrop in May 1975. (J.Wiseman)

6.48.   Our final view shows no.361 as it shunts its ancient carriage into the sidings at Cittanova, near Cinquefrondi on 12th May 1975.   (J.Wiseman)

CONCLUSION

Fortunately many of the Italian narrow gauge lines featured in this volume have survived, especially those in the south of the country. In addition, the islands of Sicily and Sardinia have both retained extensive 950mm gauge systems, which will be covered in a future volume in this series.

Italy is a regular destination of tours organised by Ffestiniog Travel, which cover many of the routes depicted within these pages. They can also arrange tours to independent requirements and provide the necessary Inter-Rail Passes - (see www.festtravel.co.uk)

Ffestiniog Travel, 6 Snowdonia Business Park, Minffordd, Gwynedd, LL48 6LD.
Tel: 01766 772050

MIDDLETON PRESS

Easebourne Lane, Midhurst, West Sussex. GU29 9AZ Tel:01730 813169

www.middletonpress.co.uk email:info@middletonpress.co.uk
A-978 0 906520 B- 978 1 873793 C- 978 1 901706 D-978 1 904474
E- 978 1 906008 F- 978 1 908174

EVOLVING THE ULTIMATE RAIL ENCYCLOPEDIA

All titles listed below were in print at time of publication - please check current availability by looking at our website - *www.middletonpress.co.uk* - or by requesting a Brochure which includes our LATEST RAILWAY TITLES also our TRAMWAY, TROLLEYBUS, MILITARY and WATERWAYS series

A
Abergavenny to Merthyr C 91 8
Abertillery and Ebbw Vale Lines D 84 5
Aberystwyth to Carmarthen E 90 1
Allhallows - Branch Line to A 62 8
Alton - Branch Lines to A 11 6
Andover to Southampton A 82 6
Ascot - Branch Lines around A 64 2
Ashburton - Branch Line to B 95 4
Ashford - Steam to Eurostar B 67 1
Ashford to Dover A 48 2
Austrian Narrow Gauge D 04 3
Avonmouth - BL around D 42 5
Aylesbury to Rugby D 91 3

B
Baker Street to Uxbridge D 90 6
Bala to Llandudno E 87 1
Banbury to Birmingham D 27 2
Banbury to Cheltenham E 63 5
Bangor to Holyhead F 01 7
Bangor to Portmadoc E 72 7
Barking to Southend C 80 2
Barmouth to Pwllheli E 53 6
Barry - Branch Lines around D 50 0
Bath Green Park to Bristol C 36 9
Bath to Evercreech Junction A 60 4
Beamish 40 years on rails E94 9
Bedford to Wellingborough D 31 9
Birmingham to Wolverhampton E253
Bletchley to Cambridge D 94 4
Bletchley to Rugby E 07 9
Bodmin - Branch Lines around B 83 1
Bournemouth to Evercreech Jn A 46 8
Bournemouth to Weymouth A 57 4
Bradshaws Guide 1866 F 05 5
Bradshaws History F18 5
Bradshaws Rail Times 1850 F 13 0
Bradshaws Rail Times 1895 F 11 6
Branch Lines series - see town names
Brecon to Neath D 43 2
Brecon to Newport E 16 6
Brecon to Newtown E 06 2
Brighton to Eastbourne A 16 1
Brighton to Worthing A 03 1
Bromley South to Rochester B 23 7
Bromsgrove to Birmingham D 87 6
Bromsgrove to Gloucester D 73 9
Broxbourne to Cambridge F16 1
Brunel - A railtour D 74 6
Bude - Branch Line to B 29 9
Burnham to Evercreech Jn B 68 0

C
Cambridge to Ely D 55 5
Canterbury - BLs around B 58 9
Cardiff to Dowlais (Cae Harris) E 47 5
Cardiff to Pontypridd E 95 6
Cardiff to Swansea E 42 0
Carlisle to Hawick E 85 7
Carmarthen to Fishguard E 66 6
Caterham & Tattenham Corner B251
Central & Southern Spain NG E 91 8
Chard and Yeovil - BLs a C 30 7
Charing Cross to Dartford A 75 8
Charing Cross to Orpington A 96 3
Cheddar - Branch Line to B 90 9
Cheltenham to Andover C 43 7
Cheltenham to Redditch D 81 4
Chester to Rhyl E 93 2
Chichester to Portsmouth A 14 7
Clacton and Walton - BLs to F 04 8
Clapham Jn to Beckenham Jn B 36 7

Cleobury Mortimer - BLs a E 18 5
Clevedon & Portishead - BLs to D180
Colonel Stephens - His Empire D 62 3
Consett to South Shields E 57 4
Cornwall Narrow Gauge D 56 2
Corris and Vale of Rheidol E 65 9
Craven Arms to Llandeilo E 35 2
Craven Arms to Wellington E 33 8
Crawley to Littlehampton A 34 5
Cromer - Branch Lines around C 26 0
Croydon to East Grinstead B 48 0
Crystal Palace & Catford Loop B 87 1
Cyprus Narrow Gauge E 13 0

D
Darjeeling Revisited F 09 3
Darlington Leamside Newcastle E 28 4
Darlington to Newcastle D 98 2
Dartford to Sittingbourne B 34 3
Derwent Valley - BL to the D 06 7
Devon Narrow Gauge E 09 3
Didcot to Banbury D 02 9
Didcot to Swindon C 84 0
Didcot to Winchester C 13 0
Dorset & Somerset NG D 76 0
Douglas - Laxey - Ramsey E 75 8
Douglas to Peel C 88 8
Douglas to Port Erin C 55 0
Douglas to Ramsey D 39 5
Dover to Ramsgate A 78 9
Dublin Northwards in 1950s E 31 4
Dunstable - Branch Lines to E 27 7

E
Ealing to Slough C 42 0
East Cornwall Mineral Railways D 22 7
East Croydon to Three Bridges A 53 6
Eastern Spain Narrow Gauge E 56 7
East Grinstead - BLs to A 07 9
East London - Branch Lines of C 44 4
East London Line B 80 0
East of Norwich - Branch Lines E 69 7
Effingham Junction - BLs a A 74 1
Ely to Norwich C 90 1
Enfield Town & Palace Gates D 32 6
Epsom to Horsham A 30 7
Eritrean Narrow Gauge E 38 3
Euston to Harrow & Wealdstone C 89 5
Exeter to Barnstaple B 15 2
Exeter to Newton Abbot C 49 9
Exeter to Tavistock B 69 5
Exmouth - Branch Lines to B 00 8

F
Fairford - Branch Line to A 52 9
Falmouth, Helston & St. Ives C 74 1
Fareham to Salisbury A 67 3
Faversham to Dover B 05 3
Felixstowe & Aldeburgh - BL to D 20 3
Fenchurch Street to Barking C 20 8
Festiniog - 50 yrs of enterprise C 83 3
Festiniog 1946-55 E 01 7
Festiniog in the Fifties B 68 8
Festiniog in the Sixties B 91 6
Finsbury Park to Alexandra Pal C 02 8
Frome to Bristol B 77 0

G
Gloucester to Bristol D 35 7
Gloucester to Cardiff D 66 1
Gosport - Branch Lines around A 36 9
Greece Narrow Gauge D 72 2

H
Hampshire Narrow Gauge D 36 4
Harrow to Watford D 14 2

Harwich & Hadleigh - BLs to F 02 4
Hastings to Ashford A 37 6
Hawkhurst - Branch Line to A 66 6
Hayling - Branch Line to A 12 3
Hay-on-Wye - BL around D 92 0
Haywards Heath to Seaford A 28 4
Hemel Hempstead - BLs to D 88 3
Henley, Windsor & Marlow C77 2
Hereford to Newport D 54 8
Hertford & Hatfield - BLs a E 58 1
Hertford Loop E 71 0
Hexham to Carlisle D 75 3
Hexham to Hawick F 08 6
Hitchin to Peterborough D 07 4
Holborn Viaduct to Lewisham A 81 9
Horsham - Branch Lines to A 02 4
Huntingdon - Branch Line to A 93 2

I
Ilford to Shenfield C 97 0
Ilfracombe - Branch Line to B 21 3
Industrial Rlys of the South East A 09 3
Ipswich to Saxmundham C 41 3
Isle of Wight Lines - 50 yrs C 12 3
Italy Narrow Gauge F 17 8

K
Kent Narrow Gauge C 45 1
Kidderminster to Shrewsbury E 10 9
Kingsbridge - Branch Line to C 98 7
Kings Cross to Potters Bar E 62 8
Kingston & Hounslow Loops A 83 3
Kingswear - Branch Line to C 17 8

L
Lambourn - Branch Line to C 70 3
Launceston & Princetown C 19 2
Lewisham to Dartford A 92 5
Lines around Wimbledon B 75 6
Liverpool Street to Chingford D 01 2
Liverpool Street to Ilford C 34 5
Llandeilo to Swansea E 46 8
London Bridge to Addiscombe B 20 6
London Bridge to East Croydon A 58 1
Longmoor - Branch Lines to A 41 3
Looe - Branch Line to C 22 2
Lowestoft - BLs around E 40 6
Ludlow to Hereford E 14 7
Lydney - Branch Lines around E 26 0
Lyme Regis - Branch Line to A 45 1
Lynton - Branch Line to B 04 6

M
Machynlleth to Barmouth E 54 3
Maestog and Tondu Lines E 06 2
March - Branch Lines around B 09 1
Marylebone to Rickmansworth D 49 4
Melton Constable to Yarmouth Bch E031
Midhurst - Branch Lines of E 78 9
Mitcham Junction Lines B 01 5
Mitchell & company C 59 8
Monmouth - Branch Lines to E 20 8
Monmouthshire Eastern Valleys D 71 5
Moretonhampstead - BL to C 27 7
Moreton-in-Marsh to Worcester D 26 5
Mountain Ash to Neath D 80 7

N
Newbury to Westbury C 66 6
Newcastle to Hexham D 69 2
Newport (IOW) - Branch Lines to A 26 0
Newquay - Branch Lines to C 71 0
Newton Abbot to Plymouth C 60 4
Newtown to Aberystwyth E 41 3
North East German NG D 44 9
Northern France Narrow Gauge C 75 8

Northern Spain Narrow Gauge E 83 3
North London Line B 94 7
North Woolwich - BLs around C 65 9

O
Ongar - Branch Line to E 05 5
Oswestry - Branch Lines around E 60 4
Oswestry to Whitchurch E 81 9
Oxford to Bletchley D 57 9
Oxford to Moreton-in-Marsh D 15 9

P
Paddington to Ealing C 37 6
Paddington to Princes Risborough C819
Padstow - Branch Line to B 54 1
Peterborough to Kings Lynn E 32 1
Plymouth - BLs around B 98 5
Plymouth to St. Austell C 63 5
Pontypool to Mountain Ash D 65 4
Pontypridd to Merthyr F 14 7
Pontypridd to Port Talbot E 86 4
Porthmadog 1954-94 - BL a B 31 2
Portmadoc 1923-46 - BLa a B 13 8
Portsmouth to Southampton A 31 4
Portugal Narrow Gauge E 67 3
Potters Bar to Cambridge D 70 8
Princes Risborough - BL to D 05 0
Princes Risborough to Banbury C 85 7

R
Reading to Basingstoke B 27 5
Reading to Didcot C 79 6
Reading to Guildford A 47 5
Redhill to Ashford A 73 4
Return to Blaenau 1970-82 C 64 2
Rhyl to Bangor F 15 4
Rhymney & New Tredegar Lines E 48 2
Rickmansworth to Aylesbury D 61 6
Romania & Bulgaria NG E 23 9
Romneyrail C 32 1
Ross-on-Wye - BLs around E 30 7
Ruabon to Barmouth E 84 0
Rugby to Birmingham E 37 6
Rugby to Loughborough F 12 3
Rugby to Stafford F 07 9
Ryde to Ventnor A 19 2

S
Salisbury to Westbury B 39 8
Saxmundham to Yarmouth C 69 7
Saxony Narrow Gauge D 47 0
Seaton & Sidmouth - BLs to A 95 6
Selsey - Branch Line to A 04 8
Sheerness - Branch Line to B 16 2
Shenfield to Ipswich E 96 3
Shrewsbury - Branch Line to A 86 4
Shrewsbury to Chester E 70 3
Shrewsbury to Ludlow E 21 5
Shrewsbury to Newtown E 29 1
Sierra Leone Narrow Gauge D 28 9
Sirhowy Valley Line E 12 3
Sittingbourne to Ramsgate A 90 1
Slough to Newbury C 56 7
South African Two-foot gauge E 51 2
Southampton to Bournemouth A 42 0
Southend & Southminster BLs E 76 5
Southern France Narrow Gauge C 47 5
South London Line B 46 6
South Lynn to Norwich City F 03 1
Southwold - Branch Line to A 15 4
Spalding - Branch Lines around E 52 9
St Albans to Bedford D 08 1
St. Austell to Penzance C 67 3
Steaming through West Hants A 69 7
Stourbridge to Wolverhampton E 16 1

St. Pancras to Barking D 68 5
St. Pancras to Folkestone E 88
St. Pancras to St. Albans C 78
Stratford-u-Avon to Birmingham
Stratford-u-Avon to Cheltenham
ST the Isle of Wight A 56 7
Sudbury - Branch Lines to F 19
Surrey Narrow Gauge C 87 1
Sussex Narrow Gauge C 68 0
Swanley to Ashford B 45 9
Swansea to Carmarthen E 59 8
Swindon to Bristol C 96 3
Swindon to Gloucester D 46 3
Swindon to Newport D 30 2
Swiss Narrow Gauge C 94 9

T
Talyllyn 60 E 98 7
Taunton to Barnstaple B 60 2
Taunton to Exeter C 82 6
Tavistock to Plymouth B 88 6
Tenterden - Branch Line to A 2
Three Bridges to Brighton A 35
Tilbury Loop C 86 4
Tiverton - BLS a C 62 8
Tivetshall to Beccles D 41 8
Tonbridge to Hastings A 44 4
Torrington - Branch Lines to B 2
Towcester - BLs around E 39 0
Tunbridge Wells BLs A 32 1

U
Upwell - Branch Line to B 64 0

V
Victoria to Bromley South A 98
Vivarais Revisited E 08 6

W
Wantage - Branch Line to D 25
Wareham to Swanage 50 yrs D
Waterloo to Windsor A 54 3
Waterloo to Woking A 38 3
Watford to Leighton Buzzard D
Welshpool to Llanfair E 49 9
Wenford Bridge to Fowey C 09
Westbury to Bath B 55 8
Westbury to Taunton C 76 5
West Cornwall Mineral Rlys D 4
West Croydon to Epsom B 08 4
West German Narrow Gauge D
West London - BLs of C 50 5
West London Line B 84 8
West Wiltshire - BLs of D 12 8
Weymouth - BLs A 65 9
Willesden Jn to Richmond B 71
Wimbledon to Beckenham C 58
Wimbledon to Epsom B 62 6
Wimborne - BLs around A 97 0
Wisbech - BLs a C 01 7
Witham & Kelvedon - BLs a E 8
Woking to Alton A 59 8
Woking to Portsmouth A 25 3
Woking to Southampton A 55 0
Wolverhampton to Shrewsbury
Worcester to Birmingham D 97
Worcester to Hereford D 38 8
Worthing to Chichester A 06 2

Y
Yeovil - 50 yrs change C 38 3
Yeovil to Dorchester A 76 5
Yeovil to Exeter A 91 8

96